Rune Wisdom and Oracle

Rune
Wisdom and Oracle

Casting – Writing - Calendar

Baron Árpád von Nahodyl Neményi

Series: Altheidnische Schriften

BoD - Books on Demand, Norderstedt

Cover: Runic manuscript Historia Hialmari.

Buchbeſchreibende Angaben der Deutſchen Nationalbibliothek: Die
Deutſche Nationalbibliothek verzeichnet dieſe Veröffentlichung in
der Deutſchen Nationalbibliographie; genauere buchbeſchreibende
Angaben ſind im Weltnetz über www.dnb.de abrufbar.

Printed and published 2021 by BoD – Books on Demand,
Norderstedt, Germany
ISBN 978-3-7526-9204-4

Contents

Preface

In this book I would like to bring you closer to the runes, the magic symbols of the Germanic tribes, and to describe them in an understandable way. The historical sources are taken into account, but not quoted completely, because it is not intended to be a scientific book about runes, but an easy to understand guide. But neither should it be an esoteric book if "esotericism" simultaneously means ignoring unambiguous sources and replacing them with wild speculations. All the conclusions reached here are based on the historical primary sources which I had already quoted completely in my German book "Heilige Runen – Zauberzeichen des Nordens" (Ullstein 2004). This 464-page book was not easy to understand for those who are new to the runes, so the plan was for a long time to come out with a shorter, easier to understand book which I am doing now. Even if I largely refrain from citing the sources, the content of this book is still based on these sources and does not provide anything that contradicts the sources.

For the rune scientists the time of the runes began before not completely two millennia. The scientists are interested in the runes as phonetic signs and letters only, but not in the runes as symbols and magic characters. It is true that runes were also used as letters in these 2 millennia, comparable to the Latin ABC, and perhaps the Romans with their script were the Germanic model to do the same with the runes. But before this time there were runes as a magic symbol, and this part of runic history is incomprehensibly ignored by runic scientists until today. Yes, they even quite consciously do not speak of runes, but of "pre-runic conceptual signs"; that's why they deny that unambiguous runes are "runes" at all. I don't do that. In my 38 years of preoccupation with runes and Germanic religion and mythology I have come to the realization that some things that scientists have been defining for years can and sometimes even have to be questioned. If a single rune is found on a Bronze Age urn then I will also call this symbol a rune, especially if it is completely similar to a later rune.

I also don't want to associate the runes in any way with the 3rd Reich or dissociate them from it, because ancient Germanic cult symbols that came from the gods can't have anything to do with any political regimes of our centuries that may misuse individual symbols, this must be clear to any intelligent reader.

The point here is to provide good guidance on how to use the runes without becoming inaccurate or contradicting the sources. So this book is an essence from the traditions and builds on the existing knowledge about the runes. Only two topics remain unconsidered here, namely the use of runes in magic and the myths of the runic origin. These topics would have made the book unnecessarily expensive and are less interesting for most readers.

May the book help to get to know this interesting special field better and to get closer to the secrets of the runes and gods.

Bad Belzig, Autumn 2020

Chapter 1

The Runic Alphabets

For two millennia, the runes have been well attested as magical characters and symbols of the Germanic people, our ancestors and ancestors of most people in North America, North Europe and Au-
stralia. The Vikings who belong to the North Germanic people
brought the runes with them to America, which we can assume for
sure, even if the famous Kensington rune stone is probably fake.
Therefore the runes correspond to our mentality more than other
scripts and they fascinate us in due to the secrets associated with
them and because of their magical meaning and effectiveness. The
word "rune" means "whispered magic" and "secret" and is related
to the German word "raunen" (murmur). This not only refers to
the respective sign, but also to the associated, quietly whispered
magic which also includes the respective rune name itself.

Runes as letters were not used until the dawn of our era two millennia ago. Single short words, mostly magical names, can be found
on weapons or objects. But long before that time runes were used
as magic signs, verifiable since the Stone Age. Runic signs can already be found on urns, not as phonetic signs (letters) but as conceptual signs. So at that time a rune did not represent a letter to
read something, but it represented a whole group of related terms.

The runic science deals with the runes only as letters of the past
2000 years. But we are primarily interested in the runes as symbols
of the oracle and magic, as they were used from the beginning.

Fig. 1: Stone slab from Kylver, Gotland 350-400 our time.

Where do the runes come from? Scientists are still puzzling over this and disagreeing. Some of them suspect any southern alphabet as the original, but cannot agree which one it should have been. The native origin has also been assumed for at least some of the rune signs.

The myth as it is preserved in the Edda, the old Icelandic collection of nordic songs of gods and heroes, says that it was Odin (Woden), the god of wisdom, who invented or recognized the runes in a magical ritual, and later he taught the runes to special people too. According to the Edda the moon god Heimdallr is also considered a mediator of the runes to the people.

Because of their divine origin the runes were considered sacred symbols, and we also want to treat them accordingly. Runes are not there to be used to write down mundane things.

The runes have – similar to the letters of our current alphabet – a certain order. We know this order because there are different inscriptions where all runes are in their order. An example for this is the Kylver Stone in Gotland, Sweden. The full set of 24 runes which is found there dates to approximately AD 400 (Fig. 1). This runic alphabet was supposed to evoke the magical power of all runes. There is also a single rune word ("sueus"), which has to be read from the middle in both directions, so you can read the word "eus" ("horse"). In addition, a horse's head, which is now weathered, is carved into the stone. At the end of this runic alphabet you can see a peculiar tree symbol which has six branches on the left and eight on the right. It is interpreted as a secret reference to the sixth rune if you count backwards the runic alphabet, the rune Ehwaz ("horse"), and the eighth rune if you count forwards the runic alphabet, Wunjo ("delight", also the god Woden). Did the rune carver want the soul of the deceased here to get to Woden by horse to Valhalla?

There are many other rune finds where the entire runic alphabet can be found, e.g. Bracteate 22 from Vadstena, Östergötland, 1st half of the 6th century (Fig. 40, p. 147), as well as manuscripts from a later period listing the runic alphabets.

The older runic alphabets, which are common to all Germanic tribes, have 24 runes. Fig. 2 shows the oldest rune signs with their variants and sound values.

In Scandinavia, this runic alphabet was shortened to 16 runes in the

7th and 8th century; 8 runes were out of use in the north at this time. In England the runic alphabet was expanded to include a few runes more; but initially the old full set of 24 signs was used. When the Normans came to England they brought their runes from the shortened runic alphabet with them, which were simply added to the end of the old set of 24 runes. At first we should only deal with the old full set of 24 runes as it is even more original and contains all runes of the younger runic alphabet but has 8 runes more. In this way a more precise rune drawing is more possible. So it is easier to write today's names and terms than with the shortened runic alphabet of the Scandinavians. Incidentally, this was later supple-mented by three runes more (around the year 1000), because 19 runes were needed for the Golden Series of Numbers in the runic calendar.

Fig. 2: The oldest rune forms with their variants.

If we want to use runes it is necessary to learn about them. Each rune has a name and conceptual value, actually a whole group of concepts. The names of the runes from around the year 1000 are listed in various medieval manuscripts. From this, runic researchers have reconstructed the rune names as they existed about 2000 years ago. I am using these developed names here in this book.

A rune, like the first rune with the reconstructed name Fehu, stands for the term cattle, cattle ownership, but also for movable property, wealth, money, gold. Today it still exists as the term "fee". But in the course of time the runes got a sound value in addition to their conceptual value, like our modern letters. As a rule, the first letter of the rune name became the sound value of the rune. The rune Fehu can also mean the letter "f" if you wanted to use it for writing. In addition, each rune has a certain position in the order of the runes. The rune Fehu is the first rune in the runic alphabet (like the A in ABC); therefore this rune can simply stand for the number "1".

So each rune has three meanings and for the rune Fehu we have these:

ᚠ

1. Rune name: Fehu (cattle, goods, possessions, etc.)
2. Runic sound: f
3. Rune number: 1

Many runes also represent a Germanic deity, but this is not always clear. The 24 runes of the runic alphabet have a precisely defined order. According to the sound values of the first six runes in this set of runes, the whole runic alphabet of runes is called "Futhark" (f-u-th-a-r-k).
If you want to read a runic inscription, you read the runes according to their sounds; only if it doesn't make sense runes are interpreted according to their respective meaning group.

If we want to use runes, we have to carefully remember the 24 rune signs; to do this we need to know their respective names and terms. It would also be good if we knew their sound and their numerical value, but that is not so important for the oracle. We should learn by heart the shape of each rune, the names and meanings of the individual runes. This is not too difficult, because if you know the names of the runes, the conceptual meanings are almost self-explanatory.

The runic alphabet of 24 is divided into three groups of eight (Aettir). The younger runic alphabet also has such a subdivision, although there are no longer eight runes per group. The names handed down from the 17th century for these groups (Aettir) in the younger runic alphabet, namely Freyrs Aett, Hagals Aett and Tyrs Aett, cannot have existed in the older runic alphabet, as the fertility god Freyr was called Ingwaz at that time and the salutation "Freyr" (= Lord) was not in use. In any case, it is reasonable to assume that the groups of eight of the older runes also had names and were related to the three main gods: "Woden's eight" (the first 8 runes), "Thunaer's eight" (runes 9 to 16) and "Tius eight" (the runes 17 to 24).

The table on the next page shows the 24 runes of the elder Futhark with their names, phonetic values and numbers.

Each individual rune as a magical symbol represents something, but in many cases we do not know exactly what each rune represents.

In order to recognize the original underlying image of a rune, we have to deal with the material where the runes were carved in, the wood. Because the runes were not written but carved. Even today our word "to write" contains the word "writan", ("scratch, carve")

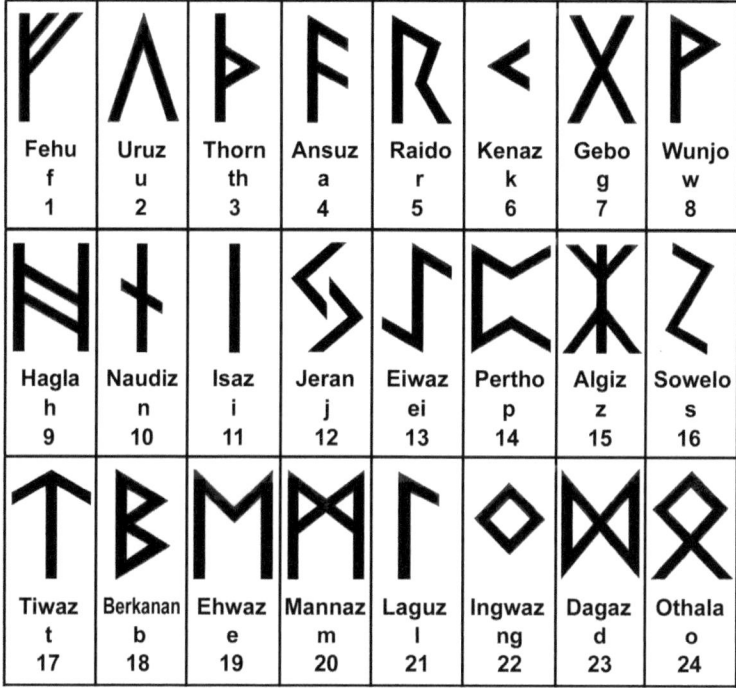

Fehu f 1	**Uruz** u 2	**Thorn** th 3	**Ansuz** a 4	**Raido** r 5	**Kenaz** k 6	**Gebo** g 7	**Wunjo** w 8
Hagla h 9	**Naudiz** n 10	**Isaz** i 11	**Jeran** j 12	**Eiwaz** ei 13	**Pertho** p 14	**Algiz** z 15	**Sowelo** s 16
Tiwaz t 17	**Berkanan** b 18	**Ehwaz** e 19	**Mannaz** m 20	**Laguz** l 21	**Ingwaz** ng 22	**Dagaz** d 23	**Othala** o 24

Fig. 3: Table of the older runic alphabet with names, numbers and sounds.

and the German term "Buchstabe" ("letter") literally means "beech stick" because the rune was carved in a stick made of beech wood. If you want to carve runes in wooden sticks you have to avoid horizontal strokes because they would run with the grain of the wood and this could split the wood. For this reason the old magical symbols were sometimes rotated by 90 degrees, i.e. placed vertically. So if we turn the rune back, we may be able to recognize the archetype on which it is based:

If we turn the first rune Fehu ᚠ 90 degrees to the left, then with a little imagination we can see a bird flying from left to right, which can be seen from the side. By the way, it is probably either an eagle or a raven, sacred birds of the god Woden. This interpretation is supported by the fact that in a Swedish rune poem the rune name of this rune is "Fugl" (= bird). But in an Icelandic rune spell the rune is characterized as an "uncut ear of wheat". So we should know that there were already different interpretations of which archetype was represented by the respective rune.

Interpretations are always uncertain; the Fehu rune can also simply represent a tree. Some scientists have interpreted the sign as a cattle head with two horns. Esoterics wanted to recognize a man with an erect phallus, etc.

For the separate meanings of the runes I will explain the traditional archetypes of the signs, provided they are convincing.

Chapter 2

Runes and Gods

The term "rune oracle" is misleading because the runes are much more than just an oracle. With the help of properly executed rune drawing we can connect with the gods. Divine powers are contained in the runes or are activated for us with the runes. That's why the idea of an actual existence of gods and spirits is necessary to understand the runes and to be able to use them for drawing lots. Because the gods give an answer only to people who include the gods in their worldview, who pray to them and ask them for answers.

In the myth as contained in the old Icelandic song collection of the Edda, it is the god Odin (Woden) who recognized or discovered the runes when he was young. Odin went to his teacher, the wise dwarf Mimir, and had to hang himself on a branch of the World Ash for 9 days and nights. He was not allowed to eat or drink. In this way a trance was induced and Odin recognized the runes in the branches below. Now he was allowed to go to earth and drink the magic potion Odroerir. The branches in which Odin recognized the runes had been spread out under the hanging god by his teacher Mimir. Odin, however, had procured the magic potion himself from the realm of the giants; that was one of his initiation tasks. But he wasn't allowed to drink the potion immediately; he just swallowed it, turned into a bird and brought it to the gods in where he spat it into prepared vessels. Because even the god had to earn the right to drink the magic potion.

Fig. 4 shows the one-eyed god Woden on the hunting frieze on the outer wall of the Königslutter church. The legend connects the hunting frieze with "Wuotan" (Wotan), that is the Old German name of the god.

People took the myth of the initiation of the god Odin as an example, and men who wanted to become rune wizards hung themselves in a similar way, sitting in a skin on a tree in the sanctuary, in order to get into a trance. They were not allowed to drink, eat, or sleep while doing this.

This is indicated by an inscription on the rune stone from Reistad, Agder, Norway, around the year 500, when the rune master called himself: "I, the awaked one [wakraz] did the carving" (see p. 138). Since "Vakr" (the awaked one) is also a name of the god Odin, staying awake seems to have been part of the initiation ritual. Fasting, which is mentioned in the Edda by Odin at his rune initiation, was probably not practiced by humans for nine days and nights, as the god did in the myth, but probably only three. In addition, the initiate was not allowed to speak.

Knock runes were allowed for necessary communications with the initiation master, a type of encoding of the runes that has been handed down in manuscripts: a first knock indicates the group of the rune, a second knock indicates its position in the group. The group often counted backwards (not always), so the 3rd rune group (beginning with Tiwaz) was considered the first. In this case the Fehu rune would be the 1st rune in the 3rd group, there is then first three taps for the group, then a short pause, and then there is one knock – this is the rune Fehu as a knock rune.

Fig. 4: Depiction of Woden on the hunting frieze on the outside of the church of Königslutter in Elm, Hannover district (Lower Saxony). Photo: H. Zippel.

After three days in the waking situation, hanging and without food or drink, strong visions arise. Such an initiation was combined with an instruction in ethical teachings; only those who have matured as a human being can learn the secret of rune magic. At the end, the initiation meditation was concluded with an admition ritual. Those who completed this ritual were allowed to call themselves "Vitki" (= wise man) or "Eruler" (unexplained, perhaps "runic knowledge-able", cf. English Earl = count) or "Thul" (runic magician who also had mythological knowledge).

In another description in the Edda we learn from the Valkyrie Sigrdrifa which rune wisdom and ethical rules taught her protégé Sigurd. Sigurd is the hero known to the German legend as Sieg-fried. He killed the dragon and got the Nibelungen treasure. Sieg-fried actually existed, it is the East Franconian King Sigibert I who was murdered in 575, but ideas of Arminius have probably also flo-wed into the legendary figure Siegfried / Sigurd.

A third story of the Edda tells us about the god Heimdallr who produces offspring with three pairs of humans from which the three classes are descended. The god teaches the runes to the son of the noble class so that he can finally become a king.

Odin (Woden) is the creator god, god of wisdom, god of souls, storms, revival and death, god of magic and ecstasy. He is still wor-shiped today in India under the name Rudra or Shiva and corre-sponds to the God-Father of Christians.

Heimdallr is the god of the moon and the god of knowledge, be-cause the moon is the first scientist, since he has to count his child-ren, the stars. Among the Germanic people he was also called Man-nus; the Indians call him Manu or Manus. From Manus comes the code of law of Manu in which the caste laws are contained. In Christianity, the god corresponds to the patriarch Noah.

If we now look at the runes of the ancient runic alphabets, at first glance we will find rune names that are identical to the names of deities:

The rune Gebo could have something to do with the love goddess Gefjon (= Freyja) or the matron Gabiae.
Wunjo (= wish) is probably related to Woden, who also has an epithet Oski (= wish, wish-fulfiller).
A connection between the rune Isaz and the goddess Isis, which the Roman Tacitus mentioned to the Germanic people, is probably absurd. But Pertho certainly has something to do with the goddess Perchta, who was mentioned as "Pertae" on a votive tablet from the Roman era by Vistre from the Nimes area. Perchta is a name of the earth and sky goddess Fria (Frigg).
Algiz refers to the divine brothers Widar and Wali, mentioned by Tacitus as Alken, Sowelo the sun goddess Sunna (Sol), Tiwaz the war god Tius (Tyr) and Bercanan the goddess Vercana (= Freyja) attested to on two Roman inscriptions (from Bad Bertrich and Ernstweiler near Zweibrücken).
Mannaz is certainly the god Mannus who in the myths of the Edda is called Heimdallr.
Ingwaz is the god Ing-Fro (Yngvi-Freyr) and Dagaz is the light god Dagr (= Baldur). In addition there is the rune Ansuz which in later times was associated with Odin, but in the older times it meant all Aesir, i.e. all gods.

So we can relate 10 of the 24 runes to deities, but with the other runes it becomes a little more difficult. Only etymological and mythological comparisons can give us an answer here.

Fig. 5: The rune stone from Stenkvista, Södermannland, Sweden around 1050 with a large Thor's hammer. State from 1916. Photo: Erik Brate.

So the name of the first rune, Fehu, could come from the Indo-European Vayu, which is a name of the wind god. Then the rune would be assigned to the wind god, Woden. The second rune denotes the primeval cattle, and since cows are dedicated to the goddess Fria (Frigg), she would be the goddess of this rune here. Fria is also the earth goddess, and this rune may represent a gateway to the underworld. Such interpretations can be made for each of the runes and thus get assignments to gods. I mention these in the chapter on runic meanings.

So the runes are firmly connected with certain gods and myths as is shown in the rune stone from Stenkvista, Södermannland, Sweden around 1050 which shows the hammer of the god Thor (Thunaer) in the middle, to invoke Thor's assistance. The runic inscription in the younger runic alphabet with partly dotted runes begins at the bottom left of the line and contains names that also refer to gods:

»Helgi auk fraykaiR auk þorkautr raistu merki siRun at þiuþ-munt faþur sin«
"Helgi and Freygeirr (= Freyrs spear) and Thorgautr (= Thor god) scratched with victory runes [this stone] after Thjodmund, their father" (the symbol "þ" represents the Th rune).

If we want to learn future things with the help of the runes, then this is only possible because the gods communicate these future things to us through the medium of the runes, provided we have carried out the questioning correctly. Neither "coincidence" (which does not exist) is involved here, nor our subconscious, nor other things. There are higher beings, deities, who guide the drawing of the runes and make us pick up the right runes exactly. The great privilege of being able to learn something from the gods, however, is not avaible for free. It is important that we offer a gift (offering) to the gods and that we create an atmosphere that helps the gods to come and to direct the drawing. In particular, any ghosts who cannot tell us anything and would at most lead us astray should be kept away. It is also known that runes were consecrated with the sign of Thor's hammer, for this reason a realistically depicted hammer was carved into some rune stones (see Fig. 5).

Incidentally, the arrangement of the runes was interpreted as referring to the inauguration paths of the three castes or classes. The first eight runes represent the path of the teaching class (Istävones), the next eight runes the nurturing class (Ingävones) and the last eight runes the soldiering class (Herminones).

ᚠ is rune of Woden, the breath coming from heaven to earth, ᚢ is the gateway to the underworld, ᚦ is the symbolic death of the person to be initiated, ᚨ is his soul and are the spirits he is supposed to know, ᚱ is the path that he now has to go, ᚲ his karma that he overcomes, ᚷ are the offerings that he now brings as a priest and ᚹ is the fulfillment of all wishes at the end of his path.

ᚺ is the rain, ᚾ the night and ᛁ the winter, forces of nature to which the farmer must expose himself, which he must know in order to obtain a good harvest ᛃ. The yew tree ᛇ is the dead tree or bow of the arrow of death which symbolically kills the person to be initiated. In the underworld he experiences the earth forces ᛈ of the earth goddess, ᛉ is his return to earth, ᛋ his life in the light of the sun.

ᛏ is the warrior candidate who must ᛒ acquire valkyries' support, ᛖ tame his horse and acquire mythological knowledge ᛗ in symbolic death. He is reborn and consecrated with water ᛚ, only now may he marry ◇ and live happily in his court as a noble ᛜ in the light ᛞ.

Chapter 3

Preparations for the Rune Drawing

If we want to do it correctly then we have to be careful about choosing the right time to make rune sticks and drawing them, finding the right place, and to include all of this in a ritual.

We want answers from the gods, so we have to go to where the gods are. According to popular belief that gods are "in heaven" or "everywhere" it would make no sense to go anywhere. Yes, gods are everywhere, even with their powers in humans, but on certain places the gods are particularly strong. The gods work in nature, and that is why their powers are there to a greater extent than elsewhere.

Admittedly, the objects in the city also originate from nature. For instance, our furniture is made of wood, and wood comes from nature. But this wood no longer lives while the wood in the forest, in the trees, is still alive. The gods are life, light, fertility, abundance, harmony. Opposed to this are the giants, i.e. beings that mean death, darkness, sterility, starvation and disharmony. Our materials processed by humans have lost their pure godly powers to a greater or lesser extent and are sometimes demonic because they have the harmful power of the giants. That is why they do not have such a high, divine vibration as untreated or only little treated natural substances. Many people still feel this and therefore they prefer to use natural, little treated materials instead of artificial, heavily processed materials (e.g. plastic). Of course, this also goes for the rune sticks.

So in nature the gods work more powerfully, they dwell there, and therefore we will celebrate all rune rituals in nature. But nature is not just nature. A field is not a forest, a pine forest is not a primeval forest, and a monoculture forest has different powers than a forest with streams, lakes or rocks. So if we just go to the next park, it's not as good as if we go to a particularly beautiful, natural forest. I think everyone has a certain sense of where nature is particularly suitable and where it is not so good. If you want to be absolutely sure, go to one of the ancient sanctuaries of our ancestors; but if there are none, e.g. in America, you can also take the holy places of the native Americans if the respective tribe allows it. Such places can easily be found with the help of legends, but also old field names or archaeological investigations. But it is also a field recorded as a place of rune drawing; it doesn't have to be an ancient sanctuary. The rune drawing must always be done outdoors because the gods are supposed to look down from heaven and influence the rune drawing.

The autumn equinox (around 9/23) is a suitable time to make the rune sticks. The eight festivals of the year or public holidays are also suitable for drawing lots. The eight festival dates are: Carnival (February 1st, Imbolc), Easter (spring equinox), May Day (May 1st, Beltene), Midsummer (summer solstice), Flax Harvest (August 1st, Lugnasad), Autumn Festival (autumn equinox), Winter Night (November 1st, Samhain, Halloween), Yule/Christmas (winter solstice). The festivals at the beginning of the month were originally full moon festivals because the month began with a full moon in ancient times. The other full moons of a year are also well suited for the rune drawing.

The right time of day is the onset of twilight in the evening. There is evidence that runes were not used during the day. Runes were found on the stone slab of Eggjum, Sogndal, Norway (dating from around 700), and the rune carver described exactly how he carved the runes. It says:

"Hasn't been struck by the sun, nor is the stone cut by a sax [short sword]. Do not lay it bare when the waning moon wanders ".

So care was taken not to use an iron tool to carve the runes and the sun should not shine; so it had to be dark and the moon shouldn't be waning.

The Roman Tacitus wrote down for us almost 2000 years ago how the rune sticks and the rune drawing were made. I want to quote this passage here literally. He writes about the Germanic people (Germania 10):

"Augury and divination by lot no people practise more diligently. The use of the lots is simple. A little bough is lopped off a fruit-bearing tree, and cut into small pieces; these are distinguished by certain marks [notae], and thrown carelessly and at random over a white garment. In public questions the priest of the particular state, in private the father of the family, invokes the gods, and, with his eyes towards heaven, takes up each piece three times, and finds in them a meaning according to the mark previously impressed on them. If they prove unfavourable, there is no further consultation that day about the matter; if they sanction it, the confirmation of augury is still required."

Even if the word "rune" is not used in the Latin text of Tacitus, we can assume that he meant runes with his "notae", which were used to designate the branch pieces.

The question is how the prayer addressed to the gods looked like;

unfortunately that is not recorded. Of course you can reformulate a prayer yourself or say a prayer freely, but we would like to know how the people in ancient times used to pray before drawing lots. There is also a prayer in the Edda (Sigrdrifumál 3f) to greet the gods which is certainly also suitable as a welcome prayer before the rune drawing:

> *"Hail Day, hail Day sons*
> *Hail Night and Nift!*
> *Look at me with loving eyes*
> *And give me praying victory.*
>
> *Hail Asir, hail Asiniar,*
> *Hail to you, good Fold!*
> *Word and wisdom grant me*
> *And healing hands always "*

Nift is one of the women of fortune, Fold is a name of the earth; the Aesir and Aesiniar are the gods and goddesses. Verses from the Edda, Hávamál 142-143 and Sigrdrifumál 16-19 are also suitable as prayer for the runic oracle.

But if we are looking for a special prayer for the rune drawing, a look at Finland can help us, because there exists the national epic Kalevala, compiled from various old mythological songs, prayers, and spells in 1835. In this Kalevala there is actually a short prayer that was said when drawing lots. Elias Lönnrot put it together from various slogans, and it is also suitable for our rune drawing. It's well known that there were many cultural contacts and influences bet-ween the North Germanics and Finns. The Finns still use the word "rune" for "verse": The "runes of Kalevala" are the verses of this poem. Germanic prayers for lots will have been very similar to these. Here are the verses from the Kalevala (IL, 77-110) where I have replaced the name of the Finnish sky god Jumala with Woden:

"Now is the time to cast the lot,
Time to consult the sign.
I ask the Creator's help
ask for a sure answer:
Speak the truth, creator sign,
Woden's lot, now let's hear it.

Speak now, lot, according to pure truth,
not according to man's wish and will,
Bring the true message
report your destiny!

If lot should lie to us
then his dignity is diminished,
It is thrown into the fire
the marks of men will be burned."

In the epic it is Väinämöinen who lays alder-lots and uses these verses along with his question. The direction of praying is always the north (looking towards the North Star).

To be able to work with runes at all, we first need the 24 rune sticks. You can't buy these anywhere; you have to make them yourself from a branch. Tacitus had written that the branch of a "fruit-bearing tree" is used for it. Well, all trees bear fruits, and they do so in autumn. So autumn is the right time to make the rune sticks, and the autumn equinox (around 9/23) is ideal. During this time the trees bear their fruits and have the most power, and we want this power for our rune sticks. Therefore, machine-made rune stones or other artificially made rune lots are only suitable for practicing and bridging the time until you have made your own rune lots. Figure 6 shows my own beechwood rune sticks.

The ritual of making the rune sticks is best started in the afternoon.

We need: A small saw, a stone as sharp-edged as possible (e.g. flint stone, lava stone) to cut, a white (undyed) cloth made of 100% linen, a pure beeswax candle, something for incense and make an offering (e.g. a piece of bread, some milk, beer, an egg).

Preparation: We should be washed and wear clothing that is as natural as possible. We must not smell unpleasant (smokers must take great care not to smoke during this time, even if it is difficult; it is necessary).

So we go to the place where we want to cut the rune sticks. Various types of wood have been handed down, spruce, fir, hazelnut, mountain ash, alder, but the most suitable are beeches. At the place where we want to perform the ritual, there should be the tree from which we want to take branches, which are easily accessible without a ladder. First we greet the gods and spirits with the prayer from the Edda already given above (page 28), while we look north. We also use this prayer as a greeting in all other rune rituals.

Then we go to the chosen tree from which we want to cut the branch. We burn incense and light the candle that we put in front of the tree. For burning incense we use collected pieces of spruce resin, which are called "pagan incense" and which have been carefully removed from the spruce tree. Dried resin can be found especially in places where branches are missing or bark is damaged. You put it on a lighted, glowing charcoal (you have to buy it in the eso-

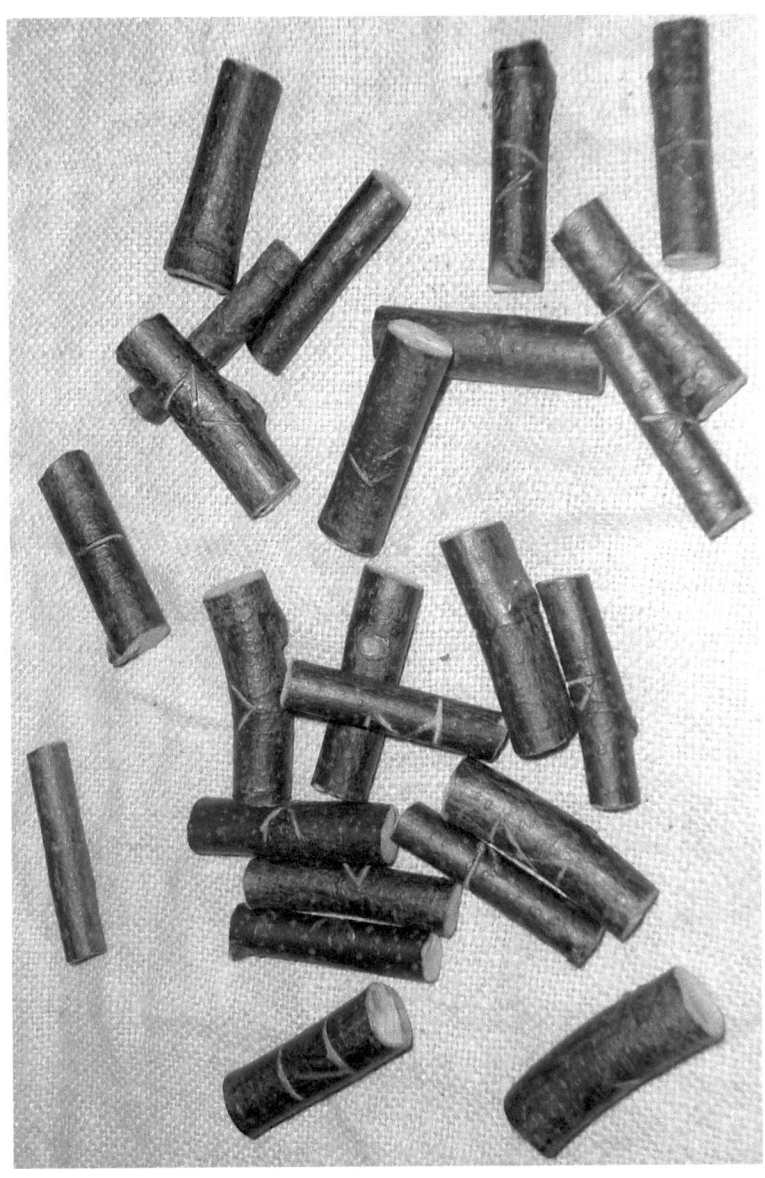

Fig. 6: Beechwood rune sticks. Photo: Árpád v. Nahodyl Neményi.

teric or church shop). When the charcoal is hot you use a censer or simply put it on a not too small, flat stone. The purpose of burning incense is to open the place for good spirits and gods, because otherwise such beings will not appear. As long as the coal is glowing we can gradually add some resin. Now we can consecrate the tree with the holy smoke, including ourselves, and the place. If that is too complicated for you, you can also buy incense cones which are usually available in stores around Christmas time. Here you should also pay attention to an odor that is as unscented as possible. Indian incense sticks with their somewhat penetrating smell are not for everyone and there is a risk that we will drive away certain spirits instead of attracting them. Because the ghosts like what comes from their region and do not know strange exotic smells.

Now we make a small sacrifice to the tree: there are very different gifts handed down: you pour some milk at the roots on the trunk, lay some bread or eggs; other gifts are also possible, e.g. Beer. We do this to reconcile the tree spirit, because we want to take a branch from the tree, and we don't want the tree spirit to get angry with us because of this, and we want to prevent that he send bad energies to the branch or to us.

You kneel down in front of the tree and ask for the chosen branch. Various prayers have been handed down about this that were said before a tree was felled; instead of "tree" you can use the tree species of the tree to which you are praying:

> *"Dear tree, give me your wood,*
> *And I'll give you mine*
> *When I've become a tree."*

So you promise the tree that one day it will get your own bones,

32

namely when you are dead and buried. In other words: we refer to the great cycle of life: we take something from nature, but nature gets our body back later.

Now we take the saw and saw off the branch that we need. It should be about a finger thick (½ inch), rather thinner, and it should be enough for 24 rune sticks, each about 1 inch long or a little longer. If it is not enough you can also saw off another branch. The sticks should be as evenly thick as possible and there shouldn't be too many knotholes, side branches, etc. Over time you would memorize certain characteristics of a stick in your subconscious, and that would not be good. All rune sticks should be as similar as possible; none should stand out in any way.

When we have the branch, we saw off 24 pieces from it. If you need two branches, you should take them from the same tree so that they contain the same power. Another tree (of the same type of tree) has a different tree spirit and you would have to offer him his own sacrifice.

On the ground in front of the tree (since the prayer direction is always north, you will sit south in front of the tree) we put the white linen cloth (about 15 x 15 to 20 x 20 inch in size) and now take one stick after the other to provide each with a rune. It may be twilight or dark; that doesn't matter, it is even helpful, because spirits awaken in the dark. We have our candle (there can be several) that give us light.

Now we take a sharp-edged stone and carve the first rune into the stick, rotated 90 degrees to the direction of the branch. This is not easy; if you are careless, the bark will split off – so proceed carefully! It would be ideal if the rune were carved in so deep that the light wood under the bark can be seen and you can feel it with your fingers in the dark. But that will be difficult, and so we should be content with a simple notch. Traditionally, this work is not done with modern iron tools, as the above-cited inscription on the Eggjum stone said. The later Icelandic rune magic also required the use of pieces of stone (there it was sharp-edged lava stone). The success of a rune spell was jeopardized if these rules were not followed. Scientists have pointed out that this rule not to carve runes with knives but with pieces of stone is an indication of the high age of the runic ritual. Because when this ritual was born there was no metal at all and you had to use pieces of stone. When the metal became known the rune ritual continued with the stone pieces, as it was feared that the new metal objects would negatively influence the result of rune drawing or rune magic. Metal is anti-demonic but it also drives away the spirits who are desired. For the same reason we only use living branches for the rune sticks, not modern materials such as plastic or artificial stone.

I have to say, however, that I had notched runes with small carving chisels because I did not always have a suitable, pointed stone and because the carving chisels worked better. In my estimation this had no negative influence on the effect of the runes; I noticed that the runes always gave clear and unambiguous answers. But if you use such small carving chisels (which are available from hobbyists), then you have to make even more effort to fill the rune sticks with force later to neutralize the remainder of negative energy of the iron. To consecrate the rune sticks with the incense also helps.

In later times, when it had already been forgotten that the power of the living, fruit-bearing tree also mattered, runes were also made in the form of planed flat wooden plates or pieces of house brand, etc. This was mostly used to draw lots for pasture or fishing grounds in the villages, so it wasn't about getting answers from the gods and that's why you don't have to be so precise.

When you have finished all 24 rune sticks you can end the ritual or – depending on the time – start the activation straight away (see the following chapter). However, this can also be done at a later time.

When we finish the ritual we say goodbye to the gods and spirits of this place with the prayer from the Edda:

> *"Safe ride, safe return*
> *Hail always!"*

Chapter 4

To fill Rune Sticks with Force

Usually there is not enough time to carry out the activation ritual immediately after the rune sticks have been made. Then our strength and attention are already weakened; we are tired, so we should do the activation as a separate ritual the next evening or later. Even if we use finished rune sticks or stones, we have to activate them magically. The respective power of the rune is to be connected to the rune stick, and we have to anchor its meaning in our consciousness.

So we go back to the place where we cut the rune sticks or to our usual place of strength, greet the gods with the prayer I already quoted above (page 28), light the candle or several beeswax candles, burn incense and put the white linen cloth in front of us on the ground (looking north). We need natural red color, for instance madder root sap, any red sap (e.g. from berries) or red earth which is applied with a little vegetable oil. With this the runic characters are colored; originally you took your own blood, which of course has more strength. I know from my own experience that it often happens that the carver injures himself and bleeds when sawing and carving, then it makes sense to use this blood for coloring.

If you actually hurt yourself more and it bleeds, then you take yarrow leaves, chew them into pulp and put them on, or the underside of a birch sponge (tree fungus). Other plant leaves that contain tannic acid also stop bleeding.

We now take the rune stick with the first rune, put it in the middle on the white cloth and sing the name of the first rune several times (i.e. "Fehu"). Then we quote the first stanza of the rune poem, in which one rune per stanza is explained. We think of the rune and its meaning and now color it red (i.e. the rune itself, not the whole stick). We have to be careful not to stain our linen. In addition, we can also recreate the runes with our bodies or trace (hit) with a magic wand in the air above the. So we do it step by step with all runes.

There are eight rune songs, i.e. old poems from the Middle Ages, which explain each rune, one after the other. Because of these rune songs we know what the runes are called and what they mean. For reasons of space I cannot list all rune songs here, but all meanings contained there are incorporated into the chapter of rune interpretation. In addition to the Old English rune poem, the other rune songs deal with the younger, shorter runic alphabet, so the Old English rune poem is best suited for the long, older rune series. In the text I have replaced the old English rune names with the reconstructed old Germanic ones:

Fehu is a comfort   to every man
yet every man   must   divide it mightily
If he will from the Drost   to redeem a judgment.

Uruz is graceful   and over-horned
A very wild animal   it fights with horns
More famous moor-stepper   a brave being.

ᚦ Thorn is exceedingly sharp,   for any knight
bad to touch,   uncommonly severe
on all men   who sit among him.

ᚨ Ansuz is the source   of all language,
wisdom carrier   and a comfort to the wise,
and every Eruler (Runemaster)   wealth and aid.

ᚱ Raido is in the hall   of any warrior
Gentle, and very hard   when they sitting on
Mighty hard mare   many miles away.

ᚲ Kenaz is known   to every living person by the fire
Pale and blinking;   often burns
Because the nobles   rest inside.

ᚷ Gebo is people's   brilliance and distinction
Prop and dignitary;   and every exile
Help and food,   who lose other things.

ᚹ Wunjo does not need,   who knows little crying,
Pain and worry,   and himself has
Luck and possessions   and enough surety too.

ᚺ Hagla is the whitest grain;
the skies whirl it,
the wind's shower walk it,
at last it melts into water.

ᚾ Naudiz presses on the chest;
it is often the case   with born men
To help and to cure,   if they hear it first.

Isaz is extremely cold,   extremely slippery;
Glitters crystal clear,   like gemstones;
A floor, wrought by the frost,   nice to look at.

Jeran is human hope,   because God allows
Holy king of heaven,   bring out the Earth's crust
Shiny grain   for the born and the poor.

Eiwaz is on the outside   a rough tree
Hard crust-proof,   keeper of fire
Strongly supported by roots,   a delight for nobles.

Pertho is alone   fun and games
of the proud   where warriors sit
In the Beer hall   happy together.

Algiz grass has Earth   more often in the fen,
Grows in water;   wounded grim,
Burns the blood   of everyone born
Who alone intends   to touch him.

Sowelo sailors   alone is a hope
When they go   over the fish's bed (= sea),
Or bring the surf stallion (= ship)   to land.

Tiwaz is a sign;   keeps loyalty well
Against the nobles;   it's on the seafaring
Over the fog of nights   never fading.

Berkanan is fruitless;   give birth right away
Branches without fruit;   it has light branches,
High in the helmet   finely equipped;
Foliage loaded   close to the air.

ᛗ *Ehwaz is for leaders   the bliss for the Nobles*
A steed, stately hoofed,   there heroes on him
Lying at ease in battle,   exchanging words
And for restlessness   is always help.

ᛗ *Mannaz in mirth   is dear to his offspring;*
Should everyone   disappear away
According to the Lord's   constant judgment
Surrender the poor flesh   to the Earth.

ᛚ *Laguz is to people   slowly thought of*
If they should dare   to stagger on boats,
And the sea wave   terrified badly
And the surf stallion   does not think of the reins.

ᛜ *Ingwaz was first   with the East Danes*
Spokesman seen   when he was east since then
Went on ways;   his car rolled after;
The Herardinge (= heroic family)   called the hero.

ᛞ *Dagaz is the Lord's messenger,   dear to men,*
The famous light Metods (= Wodan);   Joy and aid
Rich and poor,   useful to everyone.

ᛟ *Othala is loved   by every man*
Where he discusses   what is right and just
And enjoys in the building   often peace.

The poem contains some paraphrases and ancient formulations and is sometimes ambiguous, so it suits Pagans as well as Christians; the "Lord" (Drost) in stanza 1 can be the prince, but also the christian god. In the stanza to the Jeran rune, god is mentioned as the holy king of heaven, but this can refer to Woden or Fro (Freyr), too. The end of life is indicated in the stanza to the Mannaz rune; in fact, the moon god Mannus (Heimdall) watches over the gate of heaven where the souls of the dead pass. The writer of the poem still knew these mythological things, but in the Tiwaz stanza he left out the god and only described his star, the North star, by which the sailors orientated themselves. In the stanza to the Dagaz rune the name "Metod" (metering device) is used, which fits both Woden and the christian god. Most modern translations of these stanzas have unfortunately failed to recognize the ambiguity of the text.

At the end of the ritual we say goodbye to the spirits of the place as already described:

> *"Safe ride, safe return*
> *Hail always!"*

A bag made of pure, undyed linen is ideal for transporting and storing the rune sticks; a wooden box would also be possible, but it should not smell of any glue or stain. This is why an old box of this type comes into question, which no longer gives off any vapors. For the same reasons I advise against leather pouches; newly stained leather gives off a strong odor from chemical tanning agents.

Chapter 5

Process of Rune Casting

Now we have the 24 rune sticks, have a linen cloth and can finally start questioning the gods with the help of the runes, called traditionally the "rune casting".

The prerequisite for the actual rune drawing is again the necessary cultic purity. So you should abstain in the week before – but at least in the last three days before the rune drawing – of all things that pollute your own spiritual purity. These are alcohol, smoking, sexual intercourse, inharmonious music, arguments and anything that distracts from spiritual things.

The optimal time is one of the pagan annual festivals, including one of the 12-13 full moons of the year (the full moon is calculated as a period of three days). Black moon (when the moon is not visible) is sometimes already considered negative and not favorable. But since you sometimes need an answer even when there is neither a festival nor a full moon, every normal day works if necessary.

A sanctuary or any other beautiful place in nature is well suited as a place. But, as mentioned, the sources also simply contain a field (meadow).

Choose a time from dusk to night as the time of day. The bright sunny day is not suitable.

Fig. 7: Germanic priest in the thing throwing runes .

There is the tradition mentioned that runes do not get along with sunlight. Perhaps that is because certain spirits of nature, the albs (elfs), according to old belief, turn to stone during the day (actually they go into the stone where they live) and work at night only. But spirit beings are mediators to the gods, and therefore their help is also necessary.

We want help from the gods and spirits, namely answers to our questions. So we also have to give something back to the spiritual forces. "A gift always wants retribution" the god Woden tells us in the Edda. So after we have greeted the gods and spirits (as I already described on page 28) we should first make a small sacrifice, i.e. we turn to the gods, call on them and make offerings to them and burn incense.

We sit down on the ground facing north, push leaves, twigs and the top layer of soil away and place the white cloth on this place in front of us. We also light one or more candles made of pure beeswax so that we can see anything at all.

We take all the rune sticks in both of our hands and start by saying the prayer printed on page 29 or by saying free-form prayers.

We now cast the runic sticks on the white cloth; this casting (rune casting) is just a simple dropping process. It would be good if we don't look at individual runes yet because this should not lead us in a certain direction. Now we consecrate the runes by drawing the sign of Thunaer's hammer (see figure) over them with our right hand while speaking (inscription from the Glavendrup rune stone):

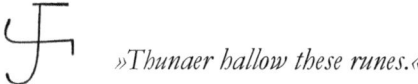 *»Thunaer hallow these runes.«*

Thunaer (Thor) is the god from whom giants, evil spirits and demons flee, and we also want to keep our runes free from such an influence. The symbol of Thunaers Hammer, handed down in a manuscript with magic symbols from Iceland (16th century), is a swastika, but has nothing to do with the Nazi regime.

Now the real rune drawing begins. Ask the most important question aloud or (if others are present who are not supposed to hear the question) in your head and, looking towards the northern sky, draw three rune sticks, one after the other. For each of the three sticks, call the name one of the Norns (women of fate), first when pulling the first stick "Wyrd" (Urd), with the second "Werdandi" (Verdandi) and with the third "Skuld" (Sculd). The names of the three Norns mean: past – what happened (became) on this matter (Wyrd

= became), present – what is happening on this matter (Werdandi = becoming), and future – what will happen, what's the results (Skuld = should, but also "debt"). We will later interpret the three runes in this sense so that the rune drawn first indicates the past, the second the present, and the third the future of the matter.

We mix the rune we have drawn with the other runes when we have recognized their symbol. We note the rune that has been drawn and then draw the next one, which we then mix in with the group of other runes. We do the same with the third rune. Theoretically, the same rune can be drawn three times in this way which underlines its importance for the answer.

If you do such a questioning for others, or if you want to make sure that you do not inadvertently see the runes before and thus influence yourself mentally, then it is advisable to use wrapped rune sticks. All 24 sticks are wrapped with a thread of pure, undyed wool. Only when a stick has been drawn do you begin to unwrap it to see the rune hidden underneath. Then the stick is wrapped again, mixed with the others and the next rune is drawn, etc.

In the Edda (Sigrdrifumál 12) wrapping is mentioned at the Thing, i.e. the court assembly of all free people, where there are many people and someone wanted to be sure that a rune drawing was not deliberately faked by the person carrying it out. It says:

> *"You should know speech runes [Málrúnar] if you want vengeance*
> *To get ahead of the enemy;*
> *Wrap around, wrap around*
> *And put them all together*
> *On the Thing where the people should*
> *Come to the complete meal."*

Fig. 8: The three Norns Skuld, Werdandi, Wyrd (from left) at the world tree.

Our whole life we are surrounded by many spirits (called "Disir") who can influence us, who protect us from dangers and who will guide our soul to the next world one day. These spirits are naturally related to the gods; they are the mediators between human beings and gods, and the three Norns also belong to the spirits who can tell us the fate that has been assigned to us in the name of the gods. In addition to the three main Norns (Wyrd, Werdandi, Skuld) there are also numerous other Norns who are involved in the allocation of fate. Unfortunately there are not only good spirits but also evil ones, at least wicked ones who want to harm us and bring us disease. The Edda calls them "Talar Disir", folk tradition "Unholds". Such beings can come to us when we live in impurity and inharmony. While we do the rune drawing, they would lead us to choose the wrong runes and we would not be able to distinguish such wrong instructions from the real ones of the gods. That is why it is very important to strictly follow the rules of purity before we cast and draw the runes.

There are doubters who argue that when you draw runes in the end only a coincidence will decide. This is not right. There is no such thing as a "coincidence". "Coincidence" is just a substitute word for certain forces that are not visible or unknown to us. The invisibility of the sequence of forces and the lack of possibility of exact repetition in practice are called "coincidence". Since there is no such thing as coincidence, it is also not coincidence that is effective in drawing lots.

The drawing of runes has nothing to do with it but is the result of invisible or unknown forces. It is our task to make sure that there are the right forces that direct our supposed "coincidence", namely the gods and good spirits, not the giants and hostile spirits.

Thoughts also play a role. It has been scientifically proven in experiments that a dice can be influenced with the help of thoughts. Our thoughts influence the result of the dice and therefore also the rune lots. But we don't really want that; we do not want to find our own thoughts in the runes, but rather answers from higher beings. That's why it is very important to control your thoughts. Especially when you draw three runes several times successively to get answers to several questions, it unfortunately happens again and again that the runes that were drawn first are still floating around in our thoughts and influence the drawing of the other runes for the other answers. Then it can happen that you draw runes again that you have already drawn. Therefore the most important question should always be asked first and preferably not another question on this day. But if you have further questions you have to try to prevent the runes that have already been drawn from dominating in your own memory. For example, it is good to recall each rune of the full rune set separately in memory so that the image of all runes is available again, and those that have already been drawed recede into the row of the other runes in our memory. Anyone who can medi-tate can try to go to the rune drawing with completely empty thoughts.

There are many other things that affect the runes, for instance the respective astronomical constellation, the weather, the respective location, etc. Therefore the place and time when and where you want to cast and draw runes are not irrelevant.

So we have now drawed three runes, one after the other by naming the names of the three Norns and memorized (or written down). Now the hardest part of the rune drawing begins, namely the inter-pretation. We relate the three runes to the time periods, so:

> 1st rune drawn: past;
> 2nd rune drawn: present;
> 3rd rune drawn: future.

You don't always ask about matters that already have a past. In such cases we follow the names of the Norns more precisely:

> 1st rune drawn: What happened in that matter?
> 2nd rune drawn: What is happening in that matter?
> 3rd rune drawn: What is the result, the answer?

Since each rune has a whole set of meanings we need to use our in-tuition to find the right meaning that fits the matter. It's not easy and it's easy to make mistakes here. Here, too, the rule of thumb is that practice creates the rune master.

You can also draw three runes without giving the drawed rune back to the other rune sticks. That means you put the three runes in front of you from right to left and start with the interpretation. Then you can never draw the same rune multiple times, but you have the advantage that you have not already seen a rune and you avoid to draw the next one with the thought of it, this would influence this drawing mentally. I used to draw according to this procedure, but then (also because of the somewhat unclear Tacitus point Germania 10) I switched to the procedure of mixing in the runes that had already been drawn and I am convinced of it today. Today I don't see the influence of the drawing of the 2nd and 3rd runes by the runes I drawed before as a problem, because it is still the same question and therefore the answer with thoughts about the question and about the respective rune can not be inappropriate.

The Germanic people also interpreted the runes in such a way that the priest made a rhyme out of the three runes, namely an alliteration in which the beginnings of the words rhyme (in German: Stabreim, that is "stave-rhyme"). The sound of the rune was used, and words that matched the rune were incorporated into the verse. This procedure is very difficult, however, because it requires real poetic skills (see page 78).

So we interpret our runes in relation to our question and, if necessary, ask further questions and draw three runes again, one after the other, etc.

Important: Don't ask "yes or no" questions. But if you want to weigh up two ways against each other, then you don't ask: "Should I do A or B?" but rather: "What will happen if I do A?" and, if necessary, as a second question: "What will happen if I do B?". And you should never ask the same thing on the same day again if you didn't like the first answer. That would be a serious disregard for the beings who let us find this first answer. And we should also be careful not to ask about mundane things. For this you can use other fortune telling methods, for example Tarot or card reading. With the runes we consult the gods, and the questions we have must be accordingly important to us.

When we have asked and answered all of our questions, we wrap the runic sticks into the white cloth, pack the bundle up and say goodbye to the beings who were invisible around us and who had inspired us, for this we use the farewell spell printed above.

We can write down the drawed runes so that we can deal with them later. But we have to start the direction of interpretation on the place where we have drawn the runes, because only under the inspiration of the spiritual beings of the place will we find the right interpretations.

If we follow the tradition of Tacitus, then no further questioning may take place on that day after a negative rune spell. Maybe we are not surrounded by good spirits after all, and other questions would also be answered negatively.
But if the answer is favorable, the rune interpretation has to be confirmed by a good omen then. Omens could be certain animals that we hear or see, certain encounters that we experience, objects that we find, etc. Only when such an omen has appeared we can be sure that what the runes indicate will also happen.

In the next chapter I list the meanings of the separate runes. These meanings are based on the names of the runes and their translations, on the descriptions of the runes in the rune poems, on the interpretations of the runic symbols themselves, on the use of the runes in rune magic, and on the mythological contexts associated with the runes.

Chapter 6

Meaning of Runes

As I said before, each rune has multiple meanings which certainly fit together in terms of content. Most runes can also be assigned to a deity (some runes are direct namens of gods). There are also higher meanings that can be used when interpreting, if one does not get any further. But first you should take the normal meanings.

There are also certain differences to the runes of the younger runic alphabet, in due to language development, indirect Christian influence, etc., runes were interpreted slightly differently than before, when paganism was still ruling. The runes were still in use in parts of Sweden until the 19th century.

For example, the first rune Fehu was probably dedicated to the god Woden, the fourth rune Ansuz referred to the Aesir, i.e. the gods and the beings of heaven. The rune Ingwaz, on the other hand, was dedicated to the god Ing-Fro (Freyr). But this rune had disappeared in the younger runic alphabet, so that the first rune was assigned to him, which means possession, gold, money, because Ing-Fro is also a god of wealth. In the younger rune alphabet Woden received the fourth rune, because he is "the Asir" par excellence. I will go into these differences in the following list.

But for the sake of clarity I would like to quote all rune songs for the first rune so that you can see what has been handed down:

1. The Anglo-Saxon rune song (10th century):

> *»Feoh is help to all living;*
> *Let every man share it mightily*
> *If he wants to redeem a judgment from the Drost [prince].«*

2. The rune song of the Edda (Rúnatalsþáttr Óðins) (the template for the main manuscript of the Codex Regius was created 1087):

> *»I know songs, no woman can do them,*
> *And not a man's mage [descendant]:*
> *Help means one thing, because it can help*
> *Against quarrels and worries and all sorrow.«*

3. Abecedarium Nordmannicum (9th century):

> *»Fe in front write.«*

4. Norwegian rune song (14th century):

> *»Fé causes quarrels between relatives;*
> *the wolf lives in the forest.«*

5. Icelandic runic rhymes (around 1300, manuscripts later):

> *»Fé is the relative quarrel and flood fire*
> *and Gravefishes Road. Gold. Fylkir.«*

6. Latin rune names (manuscript from the end of the 15th century):

> *»Aurum is gold, gold is fé,*
> *fé is a rune rod.«*

7. Old Swedish rune poem (1600):

»Få is a dispute between the relatives.«

8. Runic poem by Stjernhjelm (17th century):

»Fugle [Bird] is the relatives quarrel
Peace every quarrel,
this is fruit year.«

We see that all rune poems here describe gold, money, property: In the Anglo-Saxon rune poem everyone is supposed to distribute wealth to get honor before the prince or before God. In Odin's rune song wealth helps in all quarrels, because feuds were ended with money. The Abecedarium only mentions that the rune is the first in line (the word "write" = "carve" is in runes there). The Norwegian rune song refers to the wolf in the forest, that means outlawed robbers who have to live there because of the desire for property. The Icelandic rune poem still has mythological paraphrases, because "flood fire" is the glow of the sea and the gold in the sea, the "grave fish" is the worm that eats the dead in the grave, then the great lindworm (dragon), which is transferred the gold treasure of the Nibelungs sits. In the last two rune poems there is "roo" (actually: silence), prescription for the older "rog" (dispute). In the last rune song there is the summarized rural meaning "fertile year", which goes with the fertility god Freyr, to whom the rune was assigned later.

Here are the rune interpretations, which were created taking into account all eight rune songs, the interpretation of the rune names and symbols, and the use of runes in magic:

The rune Fehu

The rune name means "cattle" and comes from Indo-European *peku (small cattle, woolly animal, sheep) or from Indo-European *vayu (wind god). The image (turned to the left) shows a flying bird (raven, eagle) as a symbol of the wind god. The rune was also known as an uncut ear of wheat in the Viking Age.

Meaning: cattle, domesticated animals, movable property, possessions, wealth, gold, money, payment (received or also afford), fee, abundance, fertility.

Higher meaning: Wind, wind god Woden, divine invigorating breath, life, spiritual possession, thought power, breath, poetry, wisdom, ecstasy, stormy excitement, passion.

In the younger runic alphabet the rune belongs to the god of wealth, Freyr, and the seed (Swedish: frö).

Short meaning: gold, fruit year.

The rune Uruz

The rune name means "Urcattle, Aurochs" and comes from Indo-European *ura (earth) and *ugh (out). In the Viking Age the rune image was interpreted as an "entrance door" (there were no primeval cattle in the far north). At the present time the rune was also interpreted as a cow. This rune can already be found on an urn from Börnicke (7th - 6th centuries BC) (Fig. 9, p. 59).

Meaning: cattle, aurochs, strength, (damp) earth, moisture, rust, slag, mud, (spray) rain, moor, healing earth, fertility, wildness, passage, interior, matter. Old English Ur = wealth, good.

Higher meaning: Earth and sky goddess Fria (Frigg), transition to the afterlife, death gate, underworld, birth gate, origin, healing, motherliness, earth power, earthen, earthly.

Short meaning: earth power, storms, severe winter, also wealth.

The rune Thorn

The image shows a thorn on a trunk, the name means "thorn" and has its origin in the Indo-European word *(s)ter (to be rigid, stiff). Meaning: death thorn, sleep thorn, sting, death, Thurse (giant, demon of disease), inhibition, paralysis, grief, separation, negation. Termination of pregnancy, miscarriage. It is about the notorious "deathlot" testified in the sources which always means the end or the failure of an affair, or a simple negative.

Higher meaning: paralysis, numbness, underworld demon, to fall asleep. In the younger runic alphabet the rune means torment and difficult birth for women and is identified with Saturn. Saturn was considered the great misfortune.

This rune has nothing to do with the god Thor. To avoid confusion, the rune name was changed in the north to "Thurs" (giant).

Short meaning: difficult female birth, Saturn.

The rune Ansuz

The image can mean a bird or a butterfly (turned 90 degrees to the left) which is an image for the soul. The name means "Aesir" (the family of gods) and has it origin in the Indo-European *ans (breathing, soul), Old Indian asu (soul). Since the gods were also worshiped by carved pictures, which at the same time proped up the roof as pillars, the name later also meant "pillars" and "pillars of the house".

Meaning: language, speech, communication, wisdom, mouth, gods, people of the Aesir, ancestors, spirits, soul, mouth, river (the river of the dead), cult stake (idol), ash (world tree).

Higher meaning: the gods, the ancestors, liberation, the mouth (through that the soul escapes), soul, animation.

In the younger runic alphabet the rune was identified as Odin's rune (as the ruler of fate) and with Jupiter. The rune songs also describe the estuary of a river which is the river of the dead in a mythical sense, as well as haze, fog as the place of spirits and unhealthy air for the farmer.

Short meaning: unhealthy air, gods, spirits, Jupiter.

The rune Raido

The image of this rune shows a zigzag path and appears in this shape and in the familiar shape on the urn from Börnicke (Osthavelland, 7th - 6th century BC) (Fig. 9). The name Raido means "ride" and has its origin in the Indo-European ratha (to move, be excited, get up, attack, quarrel, travel, drive, carriage, ride, path).

Meaning: ride, journey, locomotion, moving, change of location, carriage, car, rider, knight, horse, path, a long way, a thing still needs time.

Higher meaning: movement, life, the afterlife and the gods.

Short meaning: way, good luck for the riders.

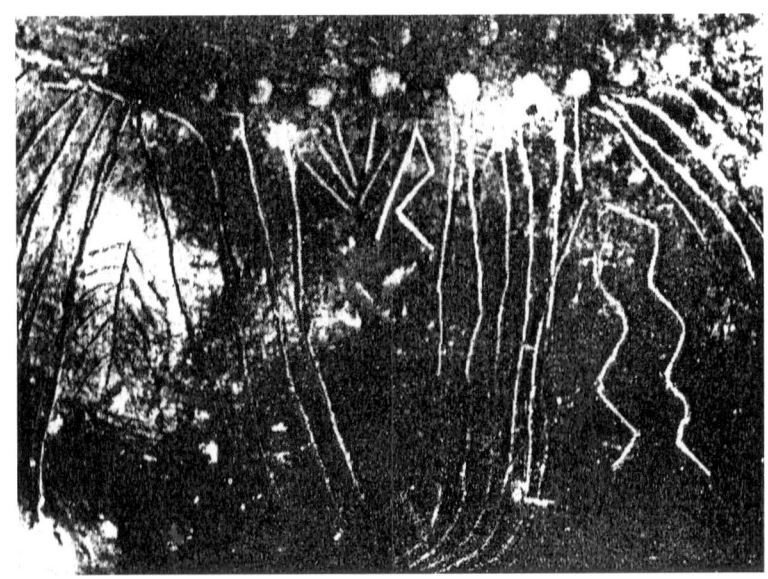

Fig. 9: Urn from Börnicke with R and U runes, 7th - 6th century BC.

The rune Kenaz

The name of the rune means "Kien, Fackel" (e.g. Kienspan, Pi-ne-span), originally Indo-European *gei (to split, break open) or Indo-European *kenis (ashes, dust). The remarkably small rune sign is supposed to represent a stylized footprint, which manifests itself in the ashes and is considered a ghost or god's trail and it is a symbol for the Karma (Ørlǫg, destiny) attached to one's own path of life. In the north the name of the rune changed to kaun (= ulcer) and to kön (= sex drive, sex, burning, heated).

Meaning: disease, ulcer, swelling, bulge, wound, crack, splitting off, ashes (of the corpse fire), coffin, pine torch, pine tree (jaw). Sex drive, burning, heated, sensuality. The interpretation is uncertain because the rune poems contradict each other.

Higher meaning: (Negative) karma that is attached to the footprint of man.

Short meaning: plague, disease, abstinence.

The rune Gebo

The name of this rune, Gebo, means "gift, present" and has its origin in the Indo-European *ghabh (to grasp, seize, receive, have, possess, bring away). The archetype is perhaps a marking cross which can already be found on Stone Age bones to mark certain annual or fixed points, the Mal Cross. The rune was removed from the younger runic alphabet.

Meaning: gift or gift received or given, offering, time of the festival of sacrifice, festival of sacrifice, gathering, dowry, special ability (gift).

Higher meaning: The goddess Gefjon ("Giver"), that is Freyja.

Short meaning: gift, festival.

The rune Wunjo

What the archetype of the rune shows is not known, possibly an ear of wheat. The name Wunjo means "bliss", Indo-European *uen(e) (= to move around, to wander, to look for something or to strive, desire, lust, joy, enjoyment). The rune name is also related to the word "wish", and the god Woden is also called "wish fulfiller" in the text sources, his walkyren "wish maide". There may also be a relationship to the name of the goddess of love Venus ("coming, growing") and the Vanes (a family of gods), whose name means "bright, shiny, shining" (wanum) or "beautiful" (vaenn). This rune does not exist in the younger rune series either.

Meaning: meadowland, meadow, wish, wish fulfilled, having wishes, bliss, comfort, lust, joy.

Higher meaning: Woden as a wish-fulfiller, Valkyries (spirits), Vanir (a special class of gods who give fertility), Venus.

Short meaning: bliss, wish fulfillment.

The rune Hagla

The name of the rune Hagla means "hail" and has its origin in the Indo-European *kaghlos (small round stone, pebbles, falling rocks, destruction). The archetype (rotated) shows the rain falling from heaven to earth. The rune developed from the Stone Age ladder symbol which means "rain", it can be found on amber pendants of the early Neolithic (5500 - 5000 BC) (Fig. 10).

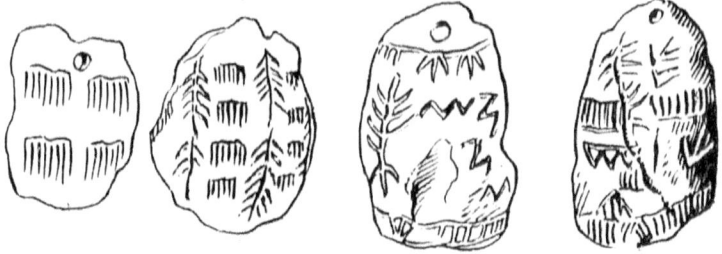

Fig. 10: Amber pendants from Denmark, early Neolithic, with rain, tree, mountain or cloud and god symbols .

It's also found on the Vandalic urn from Neubrücken, Upper Silesia around 270 BC. We can find the H rune several times next to the B or R (left), J (middle) and L rune (right) (Fig. 11).

Fig. 11: Urn from Neubrücken, Silesia around 270 years BC, with runes.

Meaning: rain, hail, hail destruction, destruction, ruin, annihilation, failure, struggle.
Higher meaning: The god Donar (god of rain, thunderstorms and hail, conqueror of giants).
Short meaning: hail, winter time, good time for the grain.

The rune Naudiz

Naudiz means "need", its Indo-European word origin is unclear, possibly it goes back to *noqt, *noku(t) (= night). The underlying archetype is also unknown, perhaps the rune represents a broken rod or a cut ear.
Meaning: hardship, coercion, desire, compulsion, coercion, bondage, oppression, suffering, poverty, misery, want, difficult situation, distress, trouble, difficulty, violence, urge.
Higher meaning: the distress will end if the distress is recognized. The rune has also been associated with the goddess who protects

the grain, Thunaer's wife Siwa (Sif), as well as with the three Norns (women of fate).

Short meaning: effort, expensive time, dearth.

The rune Isaz

This rune undoubtedly represents an icicle because its name Isaz means "ice", Indo-European *isu (= ice).

Since this rune is a simple vertical line it is not certain whether the rune is meant when we find such a line on Stone Age finds. As the rune of ice and winter, it makes sense to associate it with the winter god Wuller (Ullr).

Meaning: Ice, snow, winter, freezing, cold, cold feeling, times of need, treacherous ruin threatens (but does not necessarily have to occur), dangerous path.

Higher meaning: danger to the one for whom it is intended; it is an open question whether a particular path will be successful or not. The ice forms a bridge across the river and it is possible to break in.

Short meaning: ice, freezing cold, winter year, winter time.

The rune Jeran

This rune exists in several different variations, but all of them show two halves of a circle, as is the case in the middle on the urn from Neubrücken (Fig. 11). It represents the divided annual cycle, the change from the cold to the warm half of the year, the summer. The name Jeran means "year" and has its origin in the Indo-European *yer (year) and *jero-s (gait, run, course), meaning the course of the sun. Russian jara (= spring) and Greek hora (= hour, time, season) are also related to the name. Newer meaning: fame (Swedish: Era).

Meaning: year (as a time), good annual yield, good economic yield, summer, spring, harvest, hour, season, time.

Higher meaning: change to the good, fertility, the god Freyr brings "good year", fruitful time.

Short meaning: year, generally good.

The rune Eiwaz

The name of this rune, which denotes an intermediate between e and i, Eiwaz, means "yew", Indo-European *ei (reddish, colored). The original rune image is not known.

Since the god Wuller (Ullr), god of duels, hunting and winter, has a bow and lives in the "yew valleys", the rune has been related to him.

Meaning: yew, yew arch, hidden attack threatens, ambush, cunning, defamation, hidden opponents, poison.

Higher meaning: changing the will by keeping silent about the true intentions, seducing. The god Wuller (Ullr).

The young Swedish rune songs call the rune "minors" and denote a man who speaks on the Thing (governing assembly). The rune probably represents an opponent. Since it looks like an upside-down M rune ᛘ there: ᛧ, it is also called Stuppmadr (= fallen man).

Short meaning: Bow (enemies), hard time, dearth, expenses.

The rune Pertho

The name of this rune, Pertho, is the name of the goddess Perchta (Pertae, "the hiding one"), which corresponds to the godesses Hulda and Fria. It has its origin in the Indo-European word *bhergos (mountain, height) and *bheregh (high, sublime), but a word with the meaning "dance" was also adopted. The image of the rune shows two opposing spirals, as we often find them in prehistoric art, for instance on plate 6 of the Kivik tomb, southeast Skåne, Sweden, 1000 BC (Fig. 12).

Meaning: dance, play, joy, up and down, the course of life, fruit tree, apple tree, Old English peorth (beorth) = the born, child.

Higher meaning: Perchta (goddess of birth and death), death and rebirth, resurrection, return, hidden things.

Short meaning: The course of life, joy, child.

The rune Algiz

The name Algiz means "elk" and goes back to Indo-European *elen (deer). The image shows a moose or deer, the body is simplified here. The rune has the sound "z". From about the 5th century on it denotes the final R. The archetype can already be found on one of the rock art in the Alps (Cimbergo, Val Camonica). The Gothic word for "sanctuary" and "protection" (alhs) is related to the name. In the Old English rune poem, Elk-sedge (moose sedge, moose grass) is described because the moose was already extinct there.

Meaning: elk, deer, sun deer, defense, protection, sanctuary.

Fig. 12: Kivik tomb, Skåne, 1000 BC. Photo: Uwe Glaubach.

Higher meaning: The Alken are the divine brothers Widar and Wale (Vidar and Vali) who protect the house and sanctuary, ward off disaster, re-establish the rule of the gods after the end of the world and bring up the sun.

The rune is also known as tvimadr (two men) in the younger runic alphabet, but only on old calendars. It means cohesion, unity, and goodness.

Short meaning: protection, defense, a double golden year.

The rune Sowelo

Unfortunately, the archetype of this rune is not known, but the name Sowelo means "sun", Indo-European *sauel (sun). The sun is a goddess who also gives victory and protection to her followers.

Meaning: sun, victory, protection, summer, fertility, prosperity. Higher meaning: sun goddess, goddess of victory, knowledge of truth (the sun brings it to light).

The younger rune poems describe the sun as the highest in the sky, mention the squat in front of the sun and characterize the rune as a wheel according to the sun shape.

Short meaning: victory, summer, blue year.

The rune Tiwaz

The run name Tiwaz means "gods" and specifically the god Tius (Tyr), who is the god of war (identical to Mars) and of the people's assembly, the Thing. The name has its origin in Indo-European *deiwoz (shine, honor, day). Because the Christians didn't want to mention the pagan god, several rune poems describe the north star as the seat of the god Tius, to whom the sailors oriented themselves. A stylized representation of the face of the god is assumed to be the rune original, as it can be found on the funnel beaker from Halberstadt (2000 - 1600 before our time) (Fig. 13 left) or on the face urn from Wittenberg-Neuburg (6th or 7th century v. Ztw.) (Fig. 13, right), as well as on other urns (see also Fig. 14).

Meaning: The gods, victory, courage, honor, struggle, bravery, jewelry, activity.

Higher meaning: Tius, Mars, warriorism, movement, fame. In a poem the fire kindled in winter is mentioned, which means inflation (cost).

Fig. 13: T rune on Bronze Age urns.

Short meaning: Mars.

The rune Berkanan

Berkanan means "birch rice" or "birch". There is also a goddess of this name (inscribed: Vercana), who corresponds to Frowa (Freyja). The underlying Indo-European original word is *bher(a)g (= shine) and * bharg(as) (= radiant shine, be bright). This refers to the light-colored birch, but you cannot see any birch in the rune image. That is why the picture, turned by 90 degrees, was interpreted as a sign of the clouds (cloud mountains), as they were already shown in the Stone Age (see Fig. 10, page 61). Frowa, the goddess of love and healing, also leads the valkyries, who can be seen in the clouds.

68

"Birch" was also a name for women and young warriors.

Meaning: woman, love, art, song, music, beauty, harmony, fertility, support, health, youth, young girl, young warrior, birch, birch forest, fir.

Higher meaning: The goddess Frowa, valkyries and their support in battle, protective spirits, healing, relief of pain.

Short meaning: woman, love, the best for work.

M

The rune Ehwaz

The original rune image of the rune Ehwaz (horse) shows a stylized horse, as it can already be seen on Bronze Age rock art (Tanumshede, Sweden). A horse with the T-rune on it, which thus represents a god's steed with a deity, can be seen on the face urn from Kehrwalde, West Prussia, Bronze Age (Fig. 14). The original Indo-European word is *ekuo-s (= horse) or *ehursa (= horse). Horses were regarded as confidants of the gods and as important helpers of the people.

Abb. 14: Face urn from Kehrwalde, West Prussia.

Meaning: horse, companion, loyal friend, loyalty, power animal, helper, supporter, support force.

Higher meaning: divine power on the material level, divine assistance, horse of the gods.

Short meaning: support, friends, strength.

The rune Mannaz

The name Mannaz means "man, men, people" and has its origin in Indo-European *ma (= measure), *mn-s, *men (= consider, think, think wisely); it is also the god Mannus (Heimdallr) who created the classes of men and corresponds to the Indian Manus. Since Mannus is the god of the moon and the ancestors, the interpretation of the rune as two crescent moon juxtaposed, which later became a double ax-like symbol, seems credible.

Meaning: man, person, moon, month (period of time), ancestors, knowledge, science, wisdom, thinking, memory.

Higher meaning: moon god Mannus, ancestral knowledge, heavenly gate, death and rebirth, descendants, people.

The younger rune shape Υ was later interpreted as "three lights", as a three-armed candlestick, which is why the rune is said to imply a golden year (that is an enlightened year).

Short meaning: person, man, knowledge, wisdom.

The rune Laguz

This rune whose name Laguz means "water", Indo-European *leg (to trickle, seep), represents a spring jumping out of the ground, which we already can find on Greek coins from the 5th century BC. As a rune of water in any manifestation it has also been assigned to the god of the sea, Njordr.

Meaning: water, spring, lake, loch, lagoon, sea, dew, wealth, health, prosperity.

Higher meaning: The god Njordr, recreation, wisdom, fertility, water of life, wealth.

In the very young rune poems the run name was understood as lag (law) and interpreted in the sense of "quarrel, argument".

Short meaning: lake, water, prosperity, wisdom, law.

The rune Ingwaz

The name of the rune, Ingwaz, is clear, it denotes the god Ingwaz (Ing, Yngvi-Freyr), the god of fertility and the fire of the sun or god of warmth. The original Indo-European word is *juuen ("young"), the name also means "boy, son, descendant", Gothic Enguz = man. The original rune image is unknown; it was interpreted as a small circle symbolizing the fire on the stove. The rune is missing in the younger runic alphabet.

Meaning: fertility, peace, joy, boy, young, fire, hearth fire, growth, wealth, harvest, lover, masculine, man.

Higher meaning: The god Ing-Fro (Yngvi-Freyr), expansion, wealth, growth, fertility, peace.

Short meaning: wealth, growth, peace.

The rune Dagaz

The archetype of the rune (it lost its two horizontal lines) is a wheel cross as an image of the heavenly fire of the sun, which we often find represented in prehistoric art, for instance on plate 6 of the Kivik tomb (Fig. 12, p. 66). The name, Dagaz, means "day" and is also a name of the light god Balder. The Indo-European original word is *dhegh(o) (= burning, fire, hot time, time when the sun is burning) and *dheguhos (fire). The rune is missing in the younger runic alphabet.

Meaning: day (also as time period), light, clear time, summer, flames, fire, blaze, heavenly fire, knowledge.

Higher meaning: The god Balder (god of day and enlightenment), light as a blessing giver, hope, new beginning.

Short meaning: day, knowledge, new beginning.

The rune Othala

This rune can already be found lying down on the rock painting of Himmelstadlund (Fig. 15) with runes "brand o" and on Kivik grave slab no. 8 (1000 BC). The name Othala means "inheritance" and also "nobility"; it has its origin in the Indo-European original word *atta, *ato-s (= father). The archetype is a fence with a gate. This rune also fell away later.

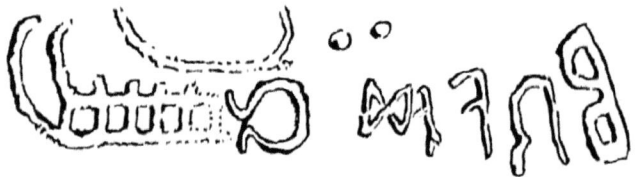

Fig. 15: Rock painting from Himmelstadlund with a lying Othala rune.

Meaning: Hereditary farm, hereditary property, family ownership of land, landed property, paternal inheritance, father, land, fatherland, house, home, sanctuary, noble court, nobility, noble.

Higher meaning: security, security and protection, being enclosed, inaccessible, seclusion.

Short meaning: house, home, legacy, nobility.

Chapter 7

Interpretation Examples

To show how drawed runes are interpreted, I used the runes to draw lots for specific topics. I want an authentic interpretation, not a constructed one, because on the one hand it is too easy, on the other hand it is also not correct, and runes might come together that make no sense for us at all. So I did a real, correct ritual with the rune sticks and used real subjects. I asked about the 4 subjects job, enemies, health, and money.

Question: Will a certain professional project be successful? The runes ᛒ Berkanan, ᛞ Dagaz and ᚲ Kenaz were drawn.
Since I asked about the future of a project that itself has no past, the first rune stands for that what just happened. It began with a fruitful activity (Berkanan), so it has good dispositions from the beginning. The second rune, Dagaz, stands for what will happen, namely the hope of good success. Unfortunately, the third rune, Kenaz, which stands for the resulting answer, doesn't seem so good: disease. The project that had a good begin will be ailing, it hasn't the success I hope for.
Therefore a additional question: What can help to achieve success, what can be done to make the project a success after all? The runes ᚺ Hagla, ᚨ Ansuz and ᛈ Pertho came. Hagla in the position of what happened means that struggle is necessary to get it better, and that can also mean that I have to discard the original idea, i.e. start a

new approach ("destroy" the previous approach, like Hail destroyed something). The second rune of the presence, Ansuz, also means that I must proceed with wisdom or prudence and better communication, then the answer of the third rune, Pertho, can be interpreted in the sense of a new beginning. It also means a fruit tree, that means the work project can actually bear fruit.

Question: Enemies harmed me. What will happen to their evil actions against me? The runes ᛏ Naudiz, ᚲ Pertho and ᚢ Uruz were drawn. Naudiz represents the past of the matter, indicating the difficult situation that the enemies have caused. Pertho stands for the present, according my interpretation these are the ups and downs. Because the enemies did not prevail, it always goes back and forth. Uruz for the future indicates it is the fate of men that it is an earthly/secular problem to be exposed to such hostilities. And it can also mean that the power of the earth can help here.

The question is: How should I respond to these attacks? The runes ᛗ Mannaz, ᛞ Dagaz and ᛁ Isaz were drawn. What happened is the bustle of the people, the human beeings, but that also means using knowledge and skills. In the presence there is the light that can overcome the malice, the light that I have to activate, but the way to create it is dangerous, the result for the future is still uncertain as the Isaz rune promises.

Question: Will a friend's financial situation improve? The runes ᛗ Ehwaz, ᛋ Sowelo and ᚷ Gebo were drawn. So what happened is the assistance of the gods and higher powers, the presence is Sowelo, a victory. The answer resulting from the past and the presence is Gebo, i.e. gift. This clearly indicates an improvement but not great wealth, because the rune Fehu should have come then.

Additional question: What must the person do to help improve their financial situation? ᚢ Uruz were drawn, ᛗ Mannaz and ᛋ

Jeran. Uruz is the earthly, material matter that should be regulated with knowledge (Mannaz) so that a good harvest (Jeran), a change to success can happen.

Question: How will the health of a related person develop? The runes ᛞ Dagaz, ᚺ Hagla and ᛖ Ehwaz were drawn. In the past it was a situation of hope (Dagaz), but now it is a destruction (Hagla), namely a bone surgery in the hospital (the god Thunaer whose rune is Hagla is also a god with his hammer something shattered; so the broken bones are meant here), but the future will bring help from supporters. In such a case you must also ask yourself why certain runes did not come, for example Kenaz for illness: Because it is not a real illness of the organs, but an orthopedic bone surgery. And why didn't Uruz come as a definite healing rune for the future? Because there will not be hundred percent healing, just mitigation.

Additional question: What can be done to improve the situation? ᛁ Isaz, ᛒ Berkanan, ᛏ Tiwaz. What happened is a difficult path (Isaz). In the presence there is support and help in relation to health (e.g. from doctors), and the answer what one can do is: develop effort and activity (Tiwaz) and don't be inactive. Berkanan is the rune of the goddess Frowa who is also a goddess of healing, and Tiwaz means here: training, because rehabilitation with gymnastics and movement training of the affected muscles is necessary due to the bone surgery and the stay in the hospital.
It is always helpful to consider why a certain perhaps clearer rune was not drawn.

There are three runes for calculating periods of time: ᛞ Dagaz (day), ᛗ Mannaz (month) and ᛃ Jeran (year, also: hour). Together with the other runes these three runes of time are a good way to ask for exact periods. The procedure used by the Germanic people how to do this is not known, but we can do it this way: For example, if you have any questions about the time when something will happen, we look at the three runes Dagaz, Mannaz and Jeran from the 24 runes. After the rune ritual we ask our question and draw only one from these three runes. Depending on which one was drawn, the period consists of days (Dagaz), months (Mannaz) or years (Jeran). When Dagaz was drawn we mix the three runes with the other runes again and then we draw one single rune: its numerical value can mean the number of days. But since there are only 24 runes, the last rune Othala must be for days 24 to 30.

But if the Mannaz rune was drawn, then the period of time will be a month. In this case we sort out the first 12 runes (Fehu to Jeran) and draw another rune from them. Your numerical value shows how many months the period of time will take. Jeran stands for 12 months or one year.

But if we had drawn the Jeran rune, the period of time will take years. Here, too, we can inquire with all runes by drawing another rune and taking its numerical value as the number of years. If the requested period of time is limited from the start, we will of course only take in fewer runes.

Example: A patient with kidney disease wants to know when he can get a new organ. The doctor says this can mean a waiting period of up to 6 years. The sick man draws the runes and the Jeran rune appears. Then, for additional question, he draws a rune from the first 6 runes only, which shows him the number of years (Fehu = 1, Uruz = 2, etc.).

Other methods are also conceivable here, how someone can use the runes to obtain precise time information for the day, month and year.

76

Fig. 16: Interpretation of runes in the home.

Important: We only draw runes in the open air, and only there we interpret the basic message. But we can then also think about it at home and work out the interpretation more precisely (Fig. 16), whereby the basic meaning found outdoors must not be canceled, even if we made a mistake in interpretation (which we did not notice at first outdoors). The spirits around us let us make this mistake without intervening, so it was studied and predetermined.

There are people who think that an upside down rune should be interpreted differently, namely negatively. I don't think so because many runes are symmetrical and you can't see whether they're upside down. But each rune stick should have its meaning and we should not neutralize this loaded meaning with a counter-meaning. There are good runes and bad ones. If we are destined to calamity we will draw a bad rune; it doesn't need a good rune which is upside down for this.

The Germanic priest method interprets runes in a rhyme. The alliteration, in German: "Stabreim" (stave rhyme), shows by its name that it was originally created with rune sticks. In the stave rhyme, a word rhymes with another, in that it begins with the same consonant or vowel (for example: "horse and hound", "bed and breakfeast" etc.). If we draw three runes (A, B, C), a stave rhyme with a long verse and a short verse emerges according to this scheme:

A A B B (also: A B A B, A B B A, B A B A, B A A B)
C C

The number of syllables is not prescribed. Runes that begin with a vowel also rhyme with other words that begin with vowel, so the runes Uruz, Ansuz, Isaz, Eiwaz, Algiz, Ehwaz, Ingwaz, Othala all rhyme, one with another.

When forming the stave rhyme, we do not have to include the names of the runes that have been drawn, but it is sufficient to keep their meaning. For example with the Mannaz rune you can rhyme: "Man is a multiplier of knowledge". The rune means man and knowledge, and the verse rhyme is on the M (man-multiplier). But it would also work without the M-alliteration: "Be the guardian of good knowledge" would also fit the M-rune meanings but with a G-alliteration. Also filler words can create a stave rhyme, the nouns do not have to rhyme with another noun always.

When asked for example about a love affair, the runes ᚢ Uruz, ᚹ Wunnjo and ᛗ Mannaz were drawn, and that could result in this alliteration:

*"Wyrd the Norn brings bliss for two lovers
Minne makes men happy. "*

78

Here the alliteration is based on the terms brings-bliss, the-two, minne-makes-men ("minne" is an old term for love, mind, memory).

Especially with stave rhymes, inspiration from the gods and spirits is particularly important, so you have to form it outdoors, where you drew the runes. And you should include the three Norns with the phases what happened, what's going to be, and debt / future. If the first drawn rune is a good love rune, then the good love affair should not be formulated for the future, but for what happened, i.e. rather the past.

You can create whole poems in this way, because if you draw three runes again, you get a long and a short verse. Together with the rhyme of the first three runes, that would be a whole stanza. Several stanzas result in a really long poem, and its content was determined by the runes.

And there is even an ancient melody that you can use to sing such verses (see my book in German language "Lieder der Vorzeit" that means "Songs of the Past").

But as I said, this Germanic priestly method is very difficult, requires a lot of practice and time and is therefore probably out of the question for most of us, unless someone is particularly poetically gifted.

For esoterics, here is an assignment of the runes to the tarot; I follow the oldest Tarot card meanings and symbols that we can for example find on the Visconti-Sforza Tarot cards (see my book in German language „Zukunftsschau mit Tarotkarten", published 2015):

0. The Fool - rune Isaz;

1. The Juggler (Magican) - rune Fehu;

2. The Popess - Rune Uruz;

3. The Empress - Rune Gebo;

4. The Emperor - Rune Jeran;

5. The Pope - Rune Wunjo;

6. The Lovers - Ingwaz rune;

7. The Chariot - Raido rune and Tiwaz rune;

8. Justice - Rune Dagaz;

9. The Hermit - Rune Kenaz;

10. The Wheel of Fortune - Pertho rune;

11. The Power - rune Ehwaz;

12. The Hanged Man - Naudiz rune;

13. Death - Rune Thorn;

14. Temperance - Berkanan rune;

15. The Devil - rune Eiwaz;

16. The House of God - Rune Hagla;

17. The Star - rune Laguz;

18. The Moon - rune Mannaz;

19. The Sun - Rune Sowelo and Rune Algiz;

20. The Judgment - rune Ansuz;

21. The World - rune Othala.

So if you draw equivocal runes but are familiar with the tarot, you can also use this knowledge for your rune interpretation by taking the tarot meaning into account.

Chapter 8

Rune Dices

It is archaeologically proven that the Germanic people used dices. They are also mentioned in the Edda (Vǫluspá 8 depending on the interpretation), and my theory is that dices evolved from the rune sticks. You can see this clearly in the dices used in the ancient game "Bell and Hammer": There are 8 dices; two of them have a bell and hammer on only one side, the other sides are blank. From the other 6 dices each one has only one number (1 to 6), and the 5 remaining sides are also blank (the sides provided with characters are shown in Fig. 17). If you cast these 6 dices, results from 0 (if no number side is up) to 21 (if all numbers are visible) are possible. This is very reminiscent of short rune sticks with only one rune sign that you draw and then see which runes appear. Perhaps dropping all the rune sticks on a cloth, where only the visible runes are interpreted, is the original rune drawing method.

My rune dices are actually ordinary dices, they just show runes instead of numbers. With three dices 18 runes are needed which requires a selection taking into account the younger, 16-character runic alphabet which is supplemented with two runes from the older runic alphabet. Even in Odin's rune song we find stanzas for 18 runes, so that we can adopt this selection.

If we want to make these dices, then a corresponding strip of the same thickness and width is sufficient, from which we saw off

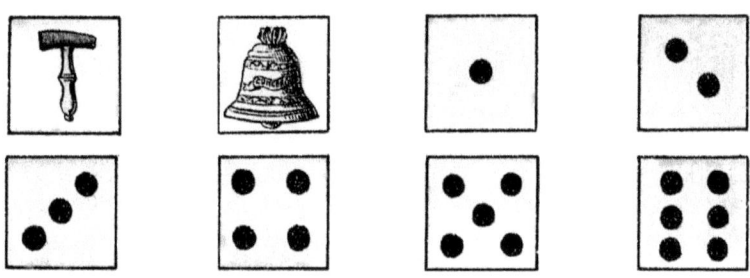

Abb. 17: The dice sides of the Bell and Hammer game.

three pieces. Since sawing work is not everyone's cup of tea, you can also buy blank wooden dices in the toy store; these are ordinary dices without numbers or other signs. You can draw the runes on the sides with a pencil, or you can carve the runes in.

When marking you follow the order of the numbers of ordinary dices, i.e. on the first dice (runes Fehu, Uruz, Thorn, Ansuz, Raido, Kenaz) you carve the 1st rune Fehu into the side where the dice has the 1 usually, the 6th rune Kenaz into the side of the 6, i.e. opposite the 1st etc., as you can see in the illustration.

The 1st dice gets the runes of the first aett, i.e. :
Fehu, Uruz, Thorn, Ansuz, Raido, Kenaz.
The 2nd dice gets the runes of the 2nd aett, these are:
Hagla, Naudiz, Isaz, Jeran, Eiwaz, Sowelo.
The 3rd dice have the runes:
Tiwaz, Berkanan, Mannaz, Laguz, Ingwaz, Othala
(see Figure 18).

The three dices can also be marked with the rune signs of the younger runic alphabet, but this is not necessary.

82

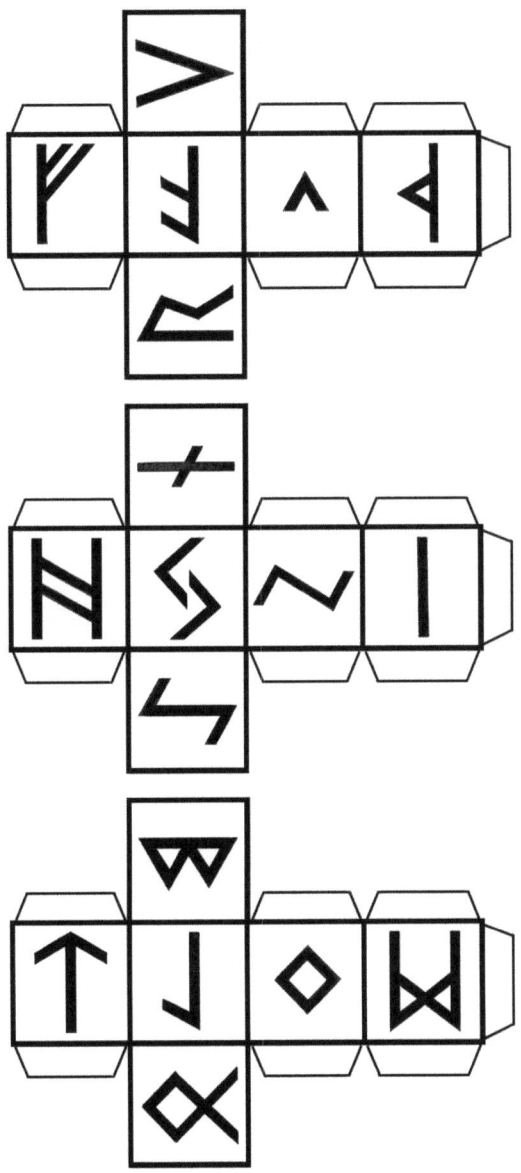

Fig. 18: Pattern for the labeling of the three rune dices.

How do you use these rune dices? You don't cast all three dice together because then you would only get runes from the three groups, but never two runes from just one of the three groups. That is why you do it outdoors, after the prayer as described in the chapter "Drawing the Runes", and after asking the question, first draw a dice without seeing it. With this dice you cast the first rune. Then you mix the dice with the others again and draw the dice for the second rune and then also for the third. In theory, the same rune can fall three times in this way; but that is not a disadvantage but an advantage, because it can make the answer even more accurate than if each rune could only be drawn once. The three runes are now interpreted according to the three Norns (Wyrd, Werdandi, Skuld) and three phases of time: past (what happened), present (what is happening) and future (what will happen, what is "owed").

The disadvantage of rune dices compared to rune sticks is that each dice has 6 runes and that's why is not filled with only one very special power. When you draw the rune sticks, the power of the stick is combined with the power that is in us and our hand, and it shows what is happening. This power connection is missing in the dice; and you don't draw the correct rune thoughtfully, but cast the dice without worrying about the power. There is a risk of using the runes on the dice like a kind of game and devaluing them. Therefore you must be careful to say the prayer and only use the dices outdoors.

The advantage of the rune dice is that you can always have them with you, e.g. when traveling, as they need little space. So quick decisions are possible. If you keep the dice in a small bag you can only draw one rune for simple things: you reach into the bag and draw a dice unseen, with which you cast the rune. The same rule here: Don't forget the prayer and never question a result by casting the dice again the same day; that would be an insult to the gods who made us find the result.

I've had the experience that the three runes drawn first influence the drawing of further runes: You still subconsciously think of the runes of the first answer and these thoughts influence the next answer. This is shown by the fact that sometimes the same runes are drawn again. Therefore, after each rune drawing it is important to imagine (visualize) all runes, one after the other, and to speak their names in your mind so that you are free from thinking about the first runes and so the next rune drawing remains unaffected. And of course you always ask the most important question first.

At the end of the questioning you say goodbye to the gods.

I found another method some years ago which has the advantage that throwing the runes only one time can give answers to all questions.

For this we use our rune sticks, not the dices. Subdivisions as shown in the figure are embroidered into the white linen cloth, but without the numbers indicated there. This division shows the medieval depiction of a astrological chart. Strictly speaking, there are three squares, a small inner one, a large outer one and a diagonal middle one placed in between. These three squares can symbolize the three worlds Asgard (the small one in the center), Midgard (the diagonal one) and Utgard (the large one at the outer edge), i.e. the world of gods, the human world, and the outer world of the giants.

After the prayer we hold all the runes about 30 cm above the center of the cloth and then we let them fall so that some runes fall or roll into the subdivisions. The runes that fall completely outside or in

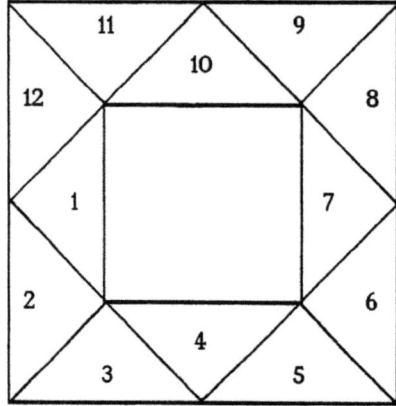

the middle are not interpreted. These 12 triangular subdivisions are the 12 astrological houses and provide answers for the subjects assigned to them. The runes of a subdivision are interpreted in the sense of the house meaning. If there is no rune in one of the fields, there is no answer for this subject. Here are the houses with their subjects, about which they provide information:

1. The Rising: birth, youth, essence, fate;
2. The Lower Gate: property, money, possession;
3. The Goddess: the fate of the siblings;
4. The Bottom of the Sky: parents, wealth, treasures of the earth;
5. Good Luck: children, births;
6. Bad Luck: poverty, diseases;
7. The Setting: spouses, end of life;
8. The Upper Gate: death, lagacies;
9. The God: religion, travel;
10. The Midheaven: fame, profession, honor;
11. The Good Demon: friends, luck;
12. The Evil Demon: enemies, suffering, prison.

First you interpret the cardines (main houses) 1, 4, 7 and 10, which are the most important. The other houses are subordinate to this.

86

Chapter 9

Runes for Writing

Runes are also letters, and we do not want to neglect this aspect of them entirely. When you draw three runes you can also read them as letters. So it is possible to read a word from the three runes. In the rune drawing example about the question of health (see Chapter 7) the runes Ehwaz, Sowelo and Gebo were drawn, i.e. the letters ESG. As with all examples in this chapter, these do not initially make any recognizable, understandable sense for us. But we know from preserved runic inscriptions that words were often shortened and runes (mostly vowels) left out, for example on the fibula from Etelhem, Gotland, Sweden from the end of the 5th century (Fig. 19). There you can only find these runes:

»**mkmrlawrtaa**«,

which is not readable at all. These runes are added in the following way: "m(i)k m(e)r(i)la w(o)rta a (...)" ("Me Merila worked A."). The "A" is the abbreviated name of the rune carver. On the stone from Rügen, Pomerania, these runes can be found: »**fgiu**« which we can complete to »f(ehu) gi(b)u« ("gift of wealth"). There are 6 runes on the buckle from Szabadbattyán, Hungary, 1st half of the 5th century: »**marŋsd**«, completed to »mar(i)ŋ s(egun) d(eda)« ("Maring blessings made"). That is why we can also add the vowels to our drawn runes, at least. ESG then becomes z. B. EaSy Go. Such a word can also be interpreted and included in the interpretation of the three runes.

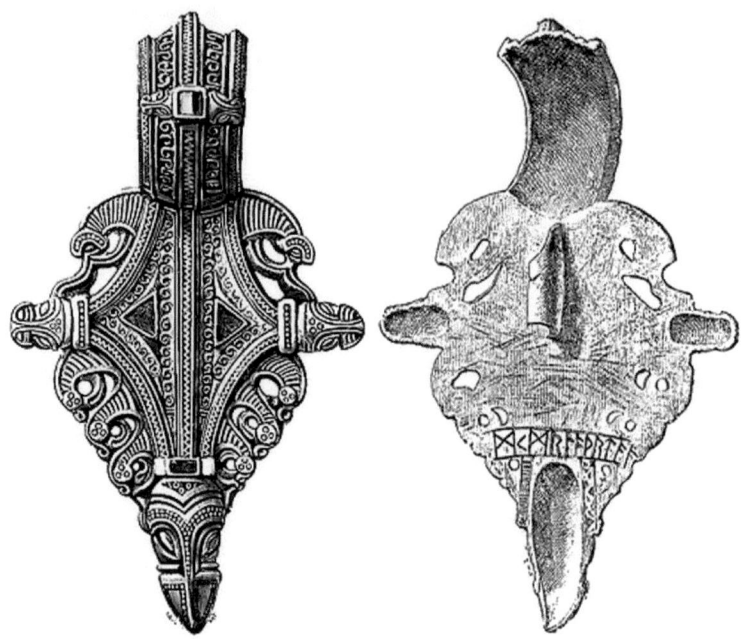

Fig. 19: Runic fibula from Etelhem, Gotland, Sweden, end of the 5th century.

If we want to use runes for writing we must bear in mind that they are magical symbols that we shouldn't misuse for mundane things. They are suitable for writing down names, magic words and spells, wishes, dreams or special spiritual experiences. If do you want to put your own name or a magic word to an object or tattoo, then note that the runes, even in one word, always retain their meaning and effect. A name that contains only runes of calamity can bring bad luck to the wearer; but single unfortunate runes can be weakened by lucky runes. If necessary, you choose a different spelling or you leave out a rune of calamity.

With runes you always write according to the sound (pronunciation) of the word, not by simply replacing latin letters with the corre-

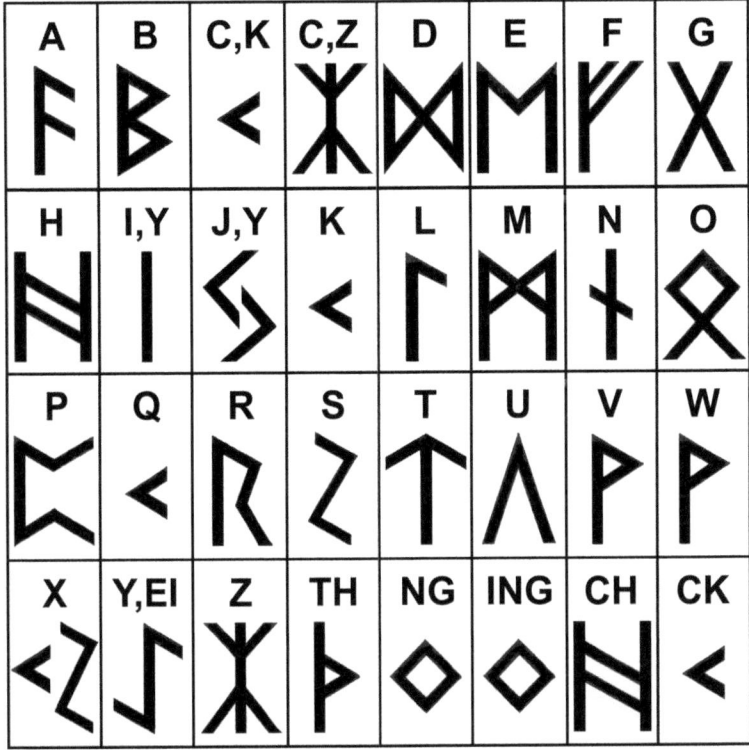

Fig. 20: Runic equivalents of our letters.

sponding runes. And as a rule, you shouldn't use double runes (the same rune doubled), unless otherwise it could lead to ambiguity. Fig. 20 lists the runes in the order of our alphabet.

A few remarks on this method: The C can sound like a Z (the first C in "circus"), then it is played with the Z rune; but if it sounds like a K (the second c in "circus" or C in "Columbia") it is expressed by the K rune. The Q is expressed by the K rune and the Qu with the K and W rune ("squash"); an X is expressed by the runes K and S

(Kenaz and Sowelo). The V is expresses by the W-rune. The Ingwaz rune has the sound NG or ING; the name "Ingo" only needs two runes, Ingwaz and Othala. The rune Eiwaz is used for the intermediate sound between E and I, but also for Y with the sound similar to an EE ("holy"). Y with the J sound ("Yen") is expressed by the Jeran rune. For the S (in "see") we have the rune Sowelo. The SCH ("School") is expressed by SK (Sowelo-Kenaz), CK only by Kenaz alone.

The rune Thorn is often used in English words ("the", "thanks"). In compound words we write T and H (Tiwaz and Hagla), for example in "penthouse".

Sometimes I observe that people tattoo the names of the gods in runes or write them down somewhere. The mistake is to write the North Germanic god names (such as Odin, Thor, etc.) of the Viking Age with the older Germanic full set of 24 runes. If you use the old runic alphabet, then of course you also have to use the god names in the older version, for example "Woden" and "Thunaer"; also the German version "Wodan", "Donar", because otherwise the runes and the gods just don't go together. But if you want to use the North Germanic names of gods from the Viking Age, then you have to use the North Germanic shortened runic alphabet. The implementation there is even more difficult because many runes represent several sounds.

In the period of time between 650 and 800 in Scandinavia, including Northern Germany, the younger runic alphabet developed from the old full set of 24 runes. The older runic alphabet still had 24 runes, but over time 8 runes were lost for the ordinary use of scripture. They were not completely forgotten but were only used for magical purposes. To write on the numerous rune stones, in the north only the shortened runic alphabet of 16 signs were used. The development of the language simply made the missing runes unnecessary. For example, the A in the north had developed more and more into an O-sound via the intermediate AO (á, å); So the Ansuz rune was used for the AO and later also for the purely O. That is why the old O rune (Othala) was no longer needed and it became superfluous.

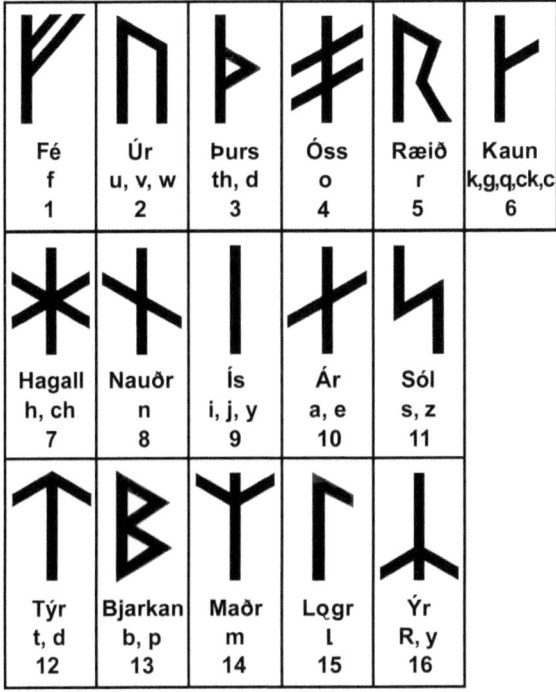

Fig. 21: The younger runes with names, sound values and numbers.

With the shortening of the runic alphabet to 16 runes, many runes were also simplified; now the runes were all designed in such a way that they only had a single vertical line, the "main stave", with the exception of the S rune and the U rune. The point was that runes standing next to each other in long inscriptions could be visually better distinguished from each other. Another reason was that so-called "One-stave runes" could be produced more easily. One-stave runes (Samstafsrunir) are several runes that are placed on top of each other on a vertical line (the main stave). The first steps in this direction were made for the older runic alphabet with the binding rune az (Ansuz above the lower part of Algiz).

The simplification of the rune signs and the formation of the younger runic alphabet containing 16 runes, which are pretty uniform in the north, presupposes the existence of a kind of committee, perhaps all the Gothis (priests) came together and decided this together. The table, Fig. 21, shows the runes of the younger runic alphabet as it was in use.

What can you do with one-stave runes? You can put names or short spells together in this way and get your own name sign, which can be used as a house or yard brand. For example, there were one-stave runes with the names of the gods Freyr and Odin and the giant Thrym (fig. 22), which should help to detect a thief.

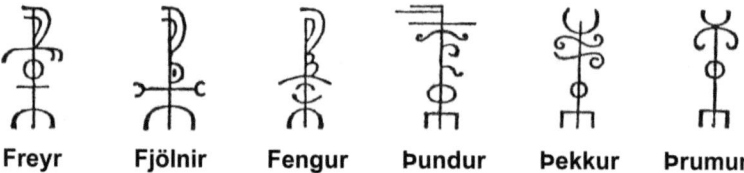

Freyr   **Fjölnir**   **Fengur**   **Þundur**   **Þekkur**   **Þrumur**

Fig. 22: One-stave runes to detect a thief.

You can put a one-stave rune together in a star shape and this increases its effect. But you can also put together several different (up to 8) one-stave runes to a star shape that form a saying; then these become magic staves.

The runes of the older runic alphabet are not suitable for one-stave runes. In the younger runic alphabet we usually have one rune for several sounds, and thus a simplification takes place when we want to convert an English word into younger runes. The most important rule is that we always follow the sound of the word and its etymology, not simply translate letter for letter into runes according to a scheme. It is well known that in the past there was no "SCH" and that is why there is no such thing with the runes. There is only the SK alone. There is no big difference between S and Z; our Z becomes S. There are also no double sounds, this is simplified and only one letter is written. I have listed the sounds in the table (Fig. 21). Because there isn't a V or W-rune we have to use the U-rune instead. The D-rune is missing, too, and so we use the TH-rune, and only a very hard D can represent the T rune. The last rune represents the ending R, which is only preserved in Nordic words, for example in the name of the god "ThorR".

If you do a one-stave rune, you should make it graphically appealing, i.e. draw the rune side branches parallel. The S-rune can be hung on the side of the main stave or the whole main stave can be "broken", i. e. the S-rune starts and continues displaced. If a second S-rune is added, it can be added replaced and so it brings the stave back to its original path. An example for this would be the name Suzanne, which we would write in runes as SUSANA and the name Susan: SUSAN.

I put the first names of my wife Catrin and myself in one-stave runes (Fig. 23). In "Catrin" the C spoken like a K is of course the K rune, the A has the E sound, in the English "Cathryn" the A is pronounced like an E or german Ä, hence the A rune. For the English name "Cathryn" we should use the TH-rune, but not for the German name "Catrin". With Árpád, on the other hand, both A's have the AO sound, hence the accents. That's why the O-rune must be there. The D at the end is rather soft here, hence the TH rune, not the T rune, and the P is of course represented by the B rune, since there is no longer a P rune in the younger runic alphabet.

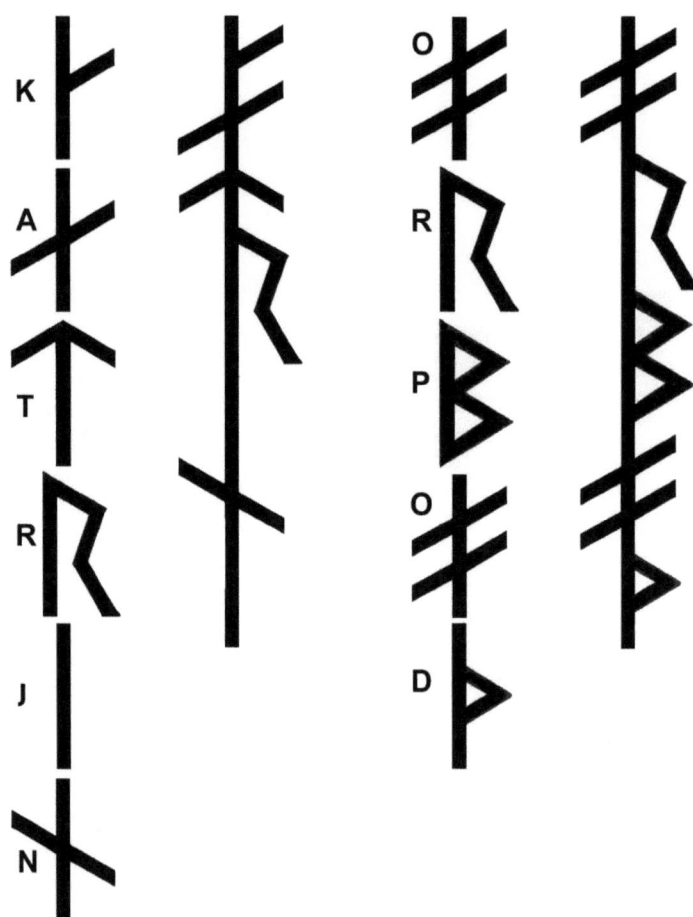

Fig. 23: The names "Catrin" and "Árpád" in one-stave runes.

94

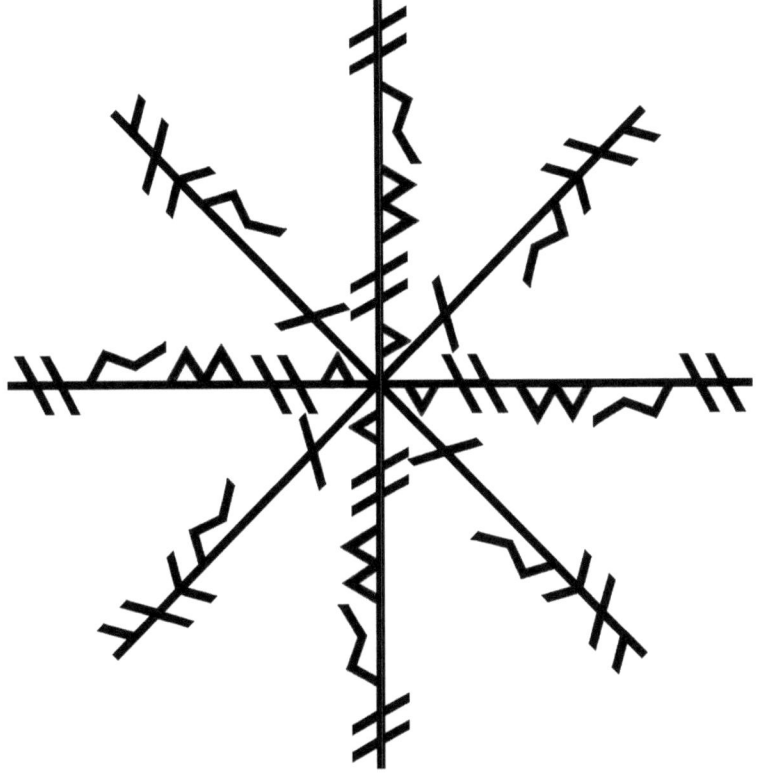

Fig. 24: One-stave runes compiled as a magic sign (Galdrastafr).

Figure 23 shows the composition of our names as individual runes and then as one-stave runes. In Figure 24, I have put together our two runes to form a magic star-shaped sign (Galdrastafr), which we e.g. can use as a symbol of luck and love. In the north, such one-stave runes were usually modified even further. Sometimes oblique lines became horizontal, or they were drawn longer or shorter, so maybe shorter at the top, longer at the bottom. Many of these one-stave runes are hardly readable for us because of their simplifications. In later times such staves like the Icelandic "Galdrastafir" (magic symbols) were created from those star-shaped staves or from differently composed staves. Codings also occur in such a way that on the left side the side branches represent the group, on the right the side branches represent the number of runes in the group. The R-rune is the 5th rune of the 3rd group, i.e. three side branches on the left and five on the right (the groups are counted from the end of the row, i.e. the runes from the T-rune are the first group). The table (page 91) also shows the numerical values of the runes.

On the so-called Erikstone from Haithabu (Hedeby), Schleswig, (2nd half of the 10th century) there are ordinary runes and at the bottom 6 single runes (Fig. 25). These result in the sentence:

ian: han: uas: sturi: matr: tregR

("and he was the helmsman").

Juxtaposed, however, they can also be read from left to right, and a further meaning arises:

i hus(i) m(a) t(reg)a a(n) at arn(i) n(i) sute

("One should complain in the house, but do not mourn at the tombstone").

It is possible that the text can also be supplemented with another meaning.

When writing rune words on objects etc. the key-runes should also be taken into account (see next chapter).

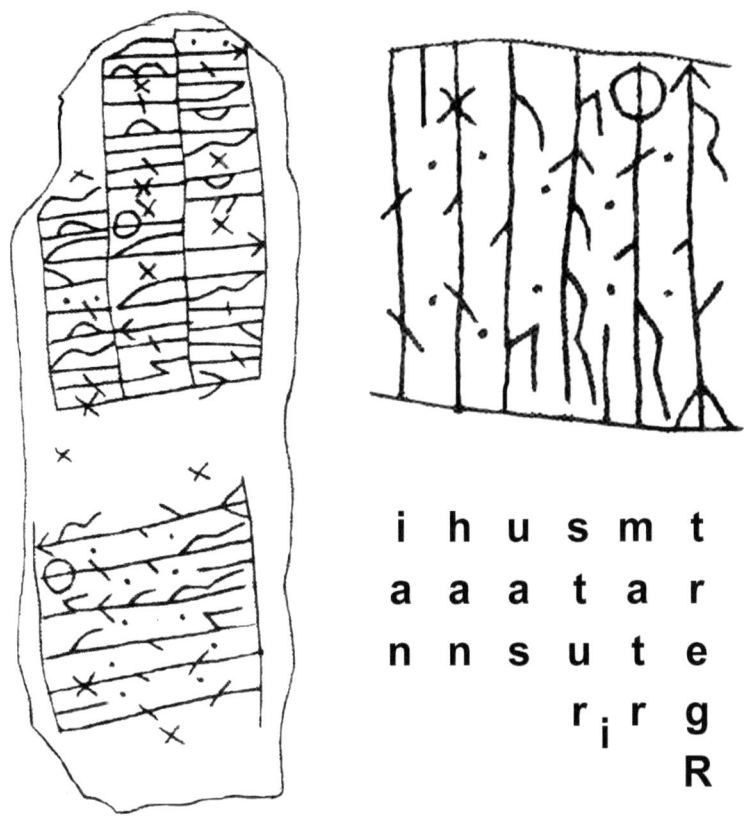

Fig. 25: The Erikstone from Haithabu, Schleswig, with one-stave runes.

One can also write with runes, using them primarily as pictorial or conceptual symbols. The phrase "The group is going home" would look like this in runes:

ᛗᛗᛗ x ᚱ x ᛟ (Mannaz-Mannaz-Mannaz - Raido - Othala). In connected terms or words where only the sound values are important, the runes are close together; but the term runes are a little further apart or separated by small crosses, high points or the like.

For the sentence "Árpád goes home" you have to write the name in vocal runs, otherwise it is not possible. That would be the runes: ᚱᚲᚾᛉ · ᚱ · ᚷ. Individual runes must be interpreted as term runes, and runes that stand together as sound runes. It is difficult to express sentences like that and to understand them, but it trains the ability to interpret.

Chapter 10

Key Runes and Name Runes

We can check a name or term that we want to write in runes on its key rune, and that works with both runic alphabets, and we usually get two different key runes then. If one of these key runes is bad and the other one is lucky, the lucky one can offset the bad one.

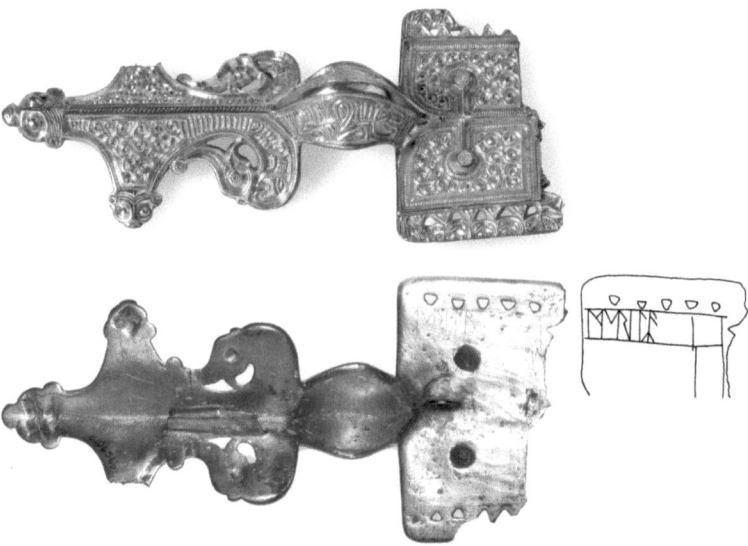

Fig. 26: Brooch from Bratsberg, Telemark, Norway, 2nd half of the 5th century with runic inscription: ekerilaz.

This method was already used by our ancestors because we find it in the runic inscription in the fibula from Bratsberg, Telemark, Norway, 2nd half of the 5th century (Figs. 26 and 27).

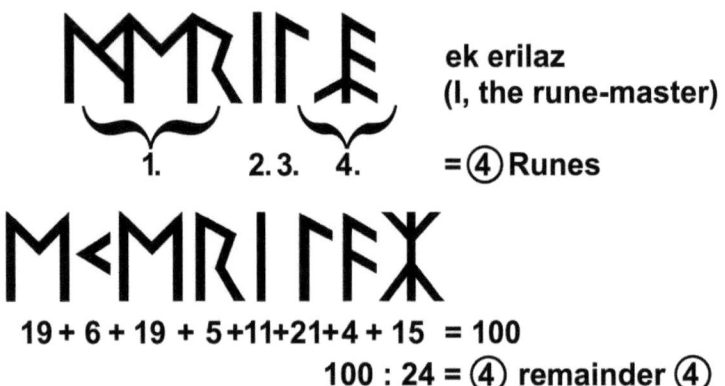

ek erilaz
(I, the rune-master)

= ④ Runes

19 + 6 + 19 + 5 +11+21+4 + 15 = 100

100 : 24 = ④ remainder ④

Fig. 27: Investigation of the Bratsberg fibula inscription.

The Bratsberg inscription consists of 4 runes: a fourfold bind rune and a one-stave rune, and two simple runes. This was done although there was enough space and the runes could have been accommodated well individually. The numerical value of all these runes is 100, and if you divide this 100 by the number of runes of the runic alphabet (namely 24), you get exactly 4 with the remainder 4. 4 runes, 4 times, remainder 4 – so the rune master has hidden the number 4 three times, the 4th rune Ansuz, the rune of the gods.

Each rune has its numerical value (see fig. 3, page 15). To find the key rune for one or more words, add the numerical values of the runes of the word – as shown in the Bratsberg example. If the value is over 24 you have to divide by 24 (number of runes in the al-

100

phabet); the remainder is the number of the key rune. If the result shows no remainder, then the remainder is 24, so the 24th rune is the key rune.

The name "Catrin" is written in the full set of 24 with the runes Kenaz + Ansuz + Tiwaz + Raido + Isaz + Naudiz, which gives the rune numbers:
$6 + 4 + 17 + 5 + 11 + 10 = 53$
This total of the rune numbers is divided by the total number of runes in the alphabet, i.e. by 24:
$53 : 24 =$ goes two times, remainder 5.
The remainder is the number of the key rune, the 5th rune Raido.

My first name Árpád is written in the full set of 24 with the following runes:
Ansuz + Raido + Pertho + Ansuz + Dagaz.
$4 + 5 + 14 + 4 + 23 = 50$
$50 : 24 = 2$, remainder 2.
So the key rune is the 2nd rune Uruz.

If we do that with the younger runes, there are nearly the same runes for the name "Catrin", but since the A in the name has the E-sound (look at the pronunciation of Cathryn in English) we must use the Ár rune: Kaun + Ár + Týr + Ræið + Ís + Nauðr. These are the numerical values:
$6 + 10 + 12 + 5 + 9 + 8 = 50$
This total of the individual runes is now divided by the whole number of runes of the younger runic alphabet, which only includes 16 runes:
$50 : 16 = 3$ times, remainder 2.
Here, too, the remainder of the rune represents the key rune, the 2nd rune, Úr (which I interpret as the rune of the goddess Frigg).

For my name Árpád in younger runes I have to use the Óss rune, since the A in the name has an O sound (which is indicated by the accents):

Óss + Ræið + Bjarkan + Óss + Þurs

The B rune here also represents the sound P which no longer has its own rune in this runic alphabet. The Th rune also represents the letter D.

4 + 5 + 13 + 4 + 3 = 29

again divided by 16 it results in 29 : 16 = 1, remainder 13.

The 13th rune in this runic alphabet is the Bjarkan rune, the rune of Freyja. If you find a rune of bad luck in your name, you should change the name or use a another first name (often you have more than just one). Or accept this burden.

These key runes can be created from any name or from several names. So you have a key rune for your first name(s), one for your surname and one for your full name that you can interpret.

The method produces the same result regardless of whether you first create the key runes from the first name and surname, then form the overall key rune from these two, or whether you add all the rune values of both names and find one overall key rune of them. If you do it name by name, you have the advantage of knowing the individual key runes of the individual names.

In the example I take the key rune of the name Catrin from the older runes, i.e. Raido, and that of my first name, Uruz. Raido is the 5th rune, Uruz the 2nd, that results in (5 + 2) 7. This number is divided by 24: 7 : 24 = 0 times, remainder 7. The 7th rune is the Gebo rune.

If you had added up all the runes of the two first names, i.e. the 50 from the name Catrin and the 53 from my name Árpád, we would get 103 (50 + 53), and 103 : 24 = 4 times, remainder 7, so we have the 7th rune Gebo, too.

The number of divisors (here the 4) certainly has a meaning too, at least the rune master of the Bratsberg fibula took this number into account. This number can also be included into a name interpretation, but ultimately it depends on the total amount of runes in the name. Of course, a very long word always has a high divisor.

The number of runes in an inscription have a special meaning too, and we find "mythical" numbers (8, 9, 12, 24, etc.) more often. For this purpose rune connections were also used, i.e. two or three runes connected in one sign, then this is counted as only one rune. The table, fig. 28, shows some of the most famous bind runes of the older runic alphabet:

Fig. 28: Bind runes of the older runic alphabet from inscriptions.

Some of these runes can also represent terms. Some bind runes can also be found on the inscriptions printed in this book. It is questionable whether their additional meanings were actually meant by the respective rune carver.

udr = wave; az = out, (on the spear of Kragehul, p. 145f or the fibula of Bratsberg, p. 99f); ga = Giving-Ase, giving god or gibu auja, give luck (on the spear of Kragehul, p. 145f); ha = hal, Hail (On the stones from Stenstad and Järsberg, page 141, or the stone from Tune, p. 144, also on the whetstone from Strøm, page 143f); he = heitir, means (on the shaft of Kragehul, p. 145f), hl = hleinir, protection; na (on Strøm's whetstone, p. 143f); er = he, the, it; what (on the Bratsberg fibula, p. 99f); ek = I (Bratsberg fibula, p. 99f); em = ek em, I am; mu = mun, lust, desire; da = Dag, Day Baldr (on the stone of Tune, p. 144 and 146) etc.

Chapter 11

Rune Postures

The so-called "rune exercises" or "rune postures", also known as "rune yoga", in which a person simulates runes with their body and sings the name of the rune, date from the previous century. They were rediscovered by the occultist and esotericist Friedrich Bernhard Marby (1882 – 1966). His critics asked to what extent such practices were actually practiced among the Germanic peoples and what evidence was there for this.

It's the runes themselves that contain hints. The Maðr rune of the younger runic alphabet means "man, human being" and actually looks like a person who raises his two arms to the side ᛘ. The same rune standing upside down bears the name Stuppmaðr, "fallen man" in the younger runic alphabet and looks like a person who does a handstand: ᛣ. It is obvious that sooner or later the pagans of the north got the idea that these runes could be simulated with the body.
In the Bosa saga, in the curse of the Busla, six curse runes are mentioned as "six men"; here the runes are identified with people.

Runes were and are sacred signs. People from today probably no longer have this thought, since runes are only one item of thousands in the esoteric supermarket today, but our ancestors had respect for runes.

The two gold horns from Gallehus, North Schleswig, which unfortunately only survive as copies, date from around 500. But there are old drawings of the originals. One horn is visibly inscribed with runes, which also contain numerical symbols. The other, supposedly "runeless" horn, on the other hand, only has different figures and pictures in its top segment. In 1969 Willi Hartner published a decryption of these little images, each image represents a rune, the same image for the same runes. It is true that we can discuss whether the decoding is actually correct in detail, but that human figures also represent runes is undisputed. Fig. 29 shows these little images and the runes they denote.

Fig. 29: Runic saying from the "runless" Gallehushorn.

You can see that the figure representing the Pertho rune is also exactly in the shape of the rune. In the figure that represents the Hagla rune, we can, with a little imagination, recognize this rune in the position of the arms and legs; it can hardly be represented better.

But in the case of the E, L and R runes there is no similarity between figures and rune shapes. But this inscription shows that already in the 5th century people were depicted sitting in the shape of runes, even if only for one or two runes. This confirms the basic idea; only the question of whether it was also done for all runes cannot be proven. With respect to the fact that the sources are incomplete, such a tradition can't be expected.

We also know from the sources that pagan images of gods were depicted with hands on hips. With this they simulate a shape of the Jeran rune.

I would also like to mention our well-known pretzel. The pretzel was traditionally baked and eaten around Easter and is associated with love, because many customs with the pretzel are customs between lovers. The name "Pretzel" or "Brecel" is identical to the name of the Bercanan rune in the form "Brica". The pretzel is just a baked form of the Bercanan rune of the goddess of love. But the pious legend ascribes the origin of the pretzel to a monk who, while baking biscuits for a fasting meal, had leftovers of dough and used it to form sausages which he interwoven so that they looked like arms folded in prayer. That's why the name "pretzel" was interpreted as Latin word "bracchium" (= forearm). This legend says that the pretzel shape represents crossed arms, and since the pretzel shape is nothing other than the Bercanan rune, this rune has been simulated with the hands, which the pious legend said in an otherwise very constructed story, because it is a contradiction in terms of baking cookies for Lent. Fasting doesn't mean just to dispense with meat.

Later in Christian times, St. Andrew appears who was crucified on an inclined cross X. I wonder why it had to be an inclined cross. But if you know that Andrew ("the male") replaced the fertility god Ing-Fro and that the inclined cross is the rune of the gift, Gebo;

Fig. 30: Runic postures for the runes of the younger runic alphabet. Left the

posture, on the right the corresponding rune (running from top to bottom).

then it makes sense. Just like the god once did, now the saint was come to give the gifts of fertility and wealth, and he was given the runic sign Gebo as an attribute. But people had to justify this in a Christian way and invented the fairy tale of the crucifixion on an inclined cross.

Runes of the older runic alphabet with several vertical lines cannot really be simulated by a single person. Perhaps one of the reasons for simplifying the runes to a vertical line, as happened from 650 onwards, was that they can be simulated more easily with the body.

In later Icelandic customs it was commonly to teach children the letters of the Latin alphabet by having them to simulate the letters with their bodies. Can't a similar method of learning assumed for the runes?

The fact that the rune names were also sung seems to be well documented by Edda verses. In the Rúnatalsþáttr of the Edda (Háv. 149, 152 and 156), for example, the god Odin mentions three runes that were sung (gel, galdr). It is now reasonable to assume that our ancestors imitated rune shapes with the body and sang the name of the respective rune with the intention to absorb or to activate the power of this rune.

Of course, the younger runic alphabet is particularly suitable for the rune postures, since each rune has only one vertical. This vertical is the body; the side branches are formed with the arms and legs. Fig. 30 shows the positions of the runes in the younger runic alphabet; you can also use these rune exercises for the corresponding runes of the older runic alphabet, because the meaning of the two alphabets differs only slightly. So if you want to put the Hagla rune you don't have to choose the old H-shaped version, which can hardly

110

be simulated, but you can choose the simplified, younger version of the rune which looks like a snow crystal and is easy to simulate by first raising and then lowering your arms during the exercise. We absorb the same force with the younger version of the rune.

There are also postures for the eight runes that are missing in the younger runic alphabet. Fig. 31 shows these postures. It should be noted that shapes were chosen for single runes that are versions of the classic shapes, but which can be easily simulated. For instance, in Fig. 31 we see a version of the Jeran rune that not only consists of two halves but looks like a diamond with a vertical line. For the Ingwaz rune, a attested version with a vertical stick has also been chosen. The sideways outstretched arms of the Dagaz rune posture bases on the fact that the Dagaz rune was originally a wheel cross which became angular in later times (square with the diagonals in it) in due to the carving technique, and so it lost the horizontal lines. So we have to imagine a circle around the whole person who simulate the rune with the body to get a sense of the wheel cross. It is not possible for just one person to take a posture that looks like the Ehwaz rune.
For the Pertho rune we find the posture that was already used for this rune on the supposedly "runless" golden horn of Gallehus. At least for this rune we can refer to a document that is 1500 years old. In these 1500 years there was no change for this rune until the rune posture at the present time.

By placing the runes with the body and repeatedly chanting their name for a long time, we absorb the respective power of the rune. While singing the rune name the assignment of tones to the planets should be taken into account; so the sowelo rune of the sun should also be sung on the musical note G (sol). The old tone assignments are:

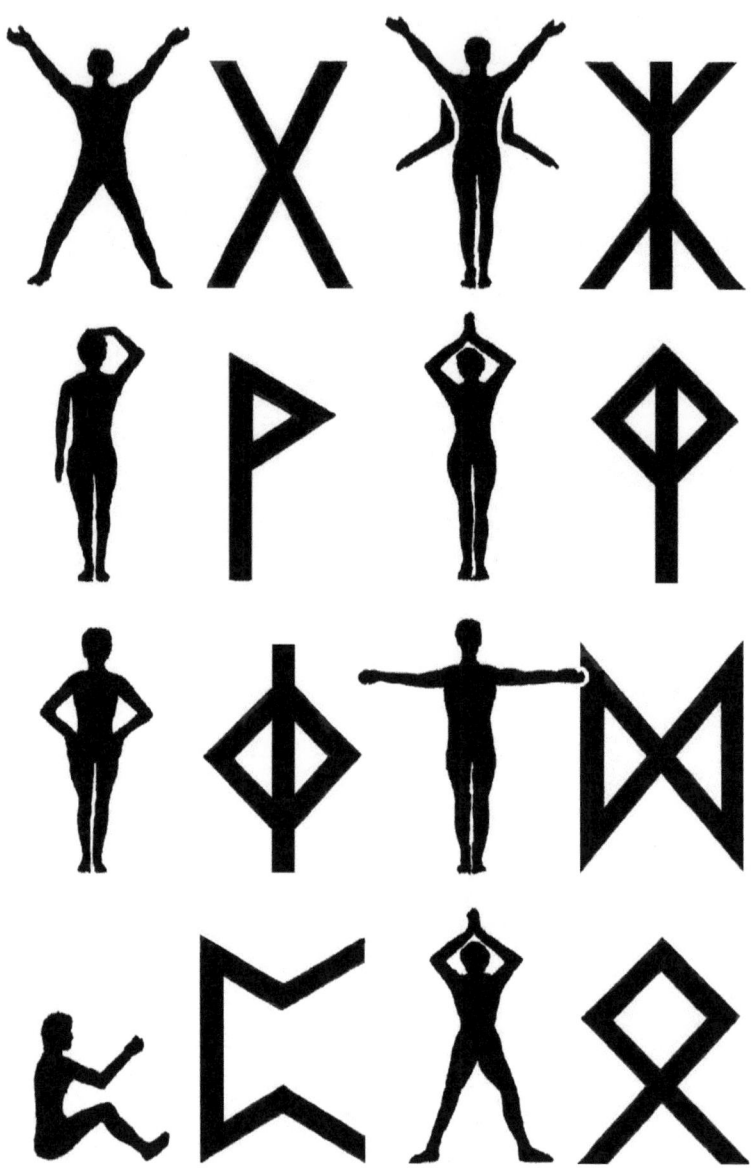

Fig. 31: Postures for the missing runes in the older runic alphabet.

112

H = Earth, C = Saturn, D = Moon, E = Mercury, F = Venus, G = Sun, A = Mars, B = Jupiter.

The runes are simulated in the open air. Depending on the rune you choose an appropriate place and, depending on the rune, turn to the sun, the moon, or look north. The names are sung for a long time, so you don't sing Fe-hu, but Feeeeoooouuuu. With runes that denote a vowel, it is also possible to sing the vowel only. If there are several participants, you can sing all runes at the same time, but it is better to sing staggered, i. e. when you have sung the name, you immediately start over with the singing of the name, regardless of whether the other participants have already finished their name. This creates a continuous sound vibration.

These are the individual rune postures in Fig. 30:

Fehu, Fé: facing the sun or the wind, both arms raised, the left one a little higher. Tone E.

Uruz, Úr: facing north with the torso bent, tone H.

Thorn, Þurs: facing east, the left hand on hips, tone C.

Ansuz, Óss: facing the wind or the north, left arm and left leg stretched forward or to the side. Tone B.

Raido, Ræið: View to the west or north, left hand on hips, left leg splayed off to the side. Tone E.

Kenaz, Kaun: looking north, both hands stretched diagonally upwards, palms down. Tone C.

Hagla, Hagall: View to the east, first Mannaz rune posture, then changing to Tiwaz posture. Or Nauðr and Ár posture, one after the other. Tone B.

Naudiz, Nauðr: View to the north, right arm points diagonally upwards, left diagonally downwards, palms accordingly. Tone H.

Isaz, Ís: Stand straight to the east or north with arms raised. It is also possible that the arms lie against the body, which is less strenuous. Tone C.

Ár: Direction of the sun, left arm points diagonally to the top left, right leg (or right arm) points diagonally down to the right. Tone F sharp.

Sowelo, Sól: Kneeling in the direction of the sun with head down. Or simulate the rune while squatting. Tone G.

Tiwaz, Týr: facing north (north star) or facing the sun or Mars, both arms spread obliquely downwards, palms facing downwards. Tone A.

Berkanan, Bjarkan: In a straight posture facing the dawn or the moon, left hand on hip, left leg bent at the knee, heel to heel, toes touching the ground (or: the sole of the left foot is on the right lower leg). Tone F.

Mannaz, Maðr: looking at the moon or north, both arms stretched upwards at the sides, forearms can also be parallel to the ground. Tone C.

Laguz, Lǫgr: look to the water or north, both arms in front of the chest pointing parallel diagonally downwards. Tone D.

Eiwaz, Ýr: looking north, upper arms laid down, forearms angled downwards at an angle, palms pointing downwards. Tone H.

About the rune postures in Fig. 31:

Gebo: looking south, legs stretched to the sides, arms raised sideways, palms facing up. Tone F.

Wunjo: facing south, right arm angled upwards. The fingers, bent down, touch the head at its top. Tone E.

Jeran: facing south, hands on hips. The right arm can also be angled upwards, as the Wunjo rune shows. Tone F sharp.

Pertho: sitting to the north and simulating the shape of the rune with arms and legs; also possible lying down. Or standing and only with the parallel arms simulating the upper part of the rune. Tone H.

Algiz: facing south, first simulating the Mannaz / Maðr rune, then changing to the Ýr rune. Or just simulating the Mannaz / Maðr rune shape. Tone G.

Ingwaz: posture straight, facing the sun, hands folded over head, palms together, wrists lightly touching the head. Tone F sharp.

Dagaz: posture straight, facing the sun, arms outstretched to the sides, palms facing forward. Or: Posture of the rune Gebo. Tone G.

Othala: view to the north, hands above the head like Ingwaz, legs stretched to the sides. Tone H.

We can also heal people with the help of the runic posture by simulating the corresponding rune that has the power that the sick person lacks and then radiating the power on the sick person with the laguz rune posture (without singing "laguz").

If you sing and simulate the runes of a whole word, one after the other, you can convey this word to the "otherworld" in this way.

If you add steps and turns to the rune postures, the rune dances emerge, which Siegfried Adolf Kummer created in the 1930s. An example:

Maðr rune dance. In a steady rhythmic step you walk in a clockwise circle with a circumference of 16 to 23 ft., which you gradually reduce. The hands are raised in the Maðr rune position and you constantly hum the sound M. Finally, you turn around in the middle in a simple twisting step, meditates on the solar plexus and the sympathetic and then tries to achieve a void of thought to receive answers or pictures (visions). You can dance in the opposite direction too. The whole dance can also be danced with the hum of "Týr", taking the Týr rune posture, or danced alternately (Maðr-Týr).

Chapter 12

Runes in the Annual Cycle

In a depiction from ancient times it is said that three nations are experienced in the interpretation of the stars and the calculation of time: Egyptians, Chaldeans and Hyperboreans. The Greeks understood the Hyperboreans as the Germanic people in the north, which they even called their teachers.

Today we know from investigations of the orientations of stone circles like Stonehenge or from finds like the Nebra Sky Disc that our ancestors watched the sky very closely and were interested in everything about the annual cycle.

The so-called Runic Almanacs or Rune staffs have survived from the Christian era (Fig. 33, p. 120); these are sword-shaped staves with runes and symbols carved onto them that served as a calendar. They were called "Allmonacht" (Almanac) because all moons of a period could be watched with it. Fig. 32 shows drawings of the runes and images from such an Almanac, the one from 1784 from Oldenburg. The oldest Almanac, the Almanac from Gotland, dates back to the year 1148. But these calendars come probably from a much older tradition. Such calendars also existed in round or oval shapes, often with notches instead of runes. At the end of an Almanac there are runes and special staves which represent numbers, for the annual calculation.

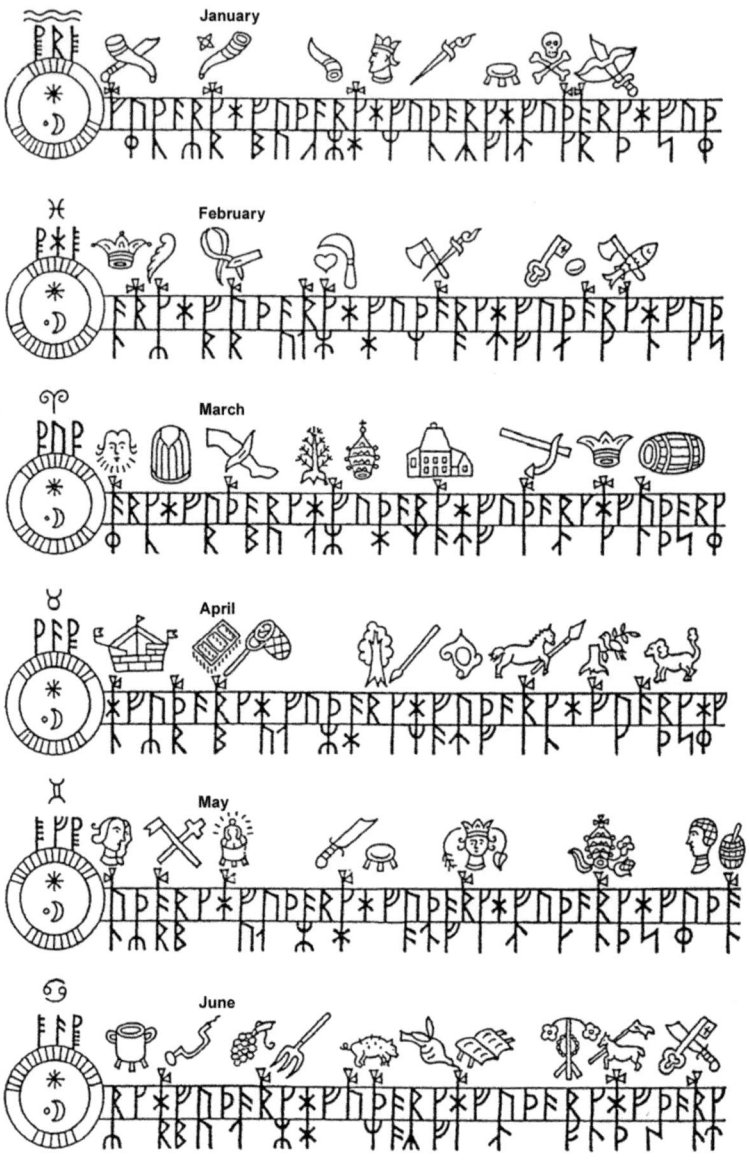

Fig. 32: Redrawing the images of the Runic Almanac from 1784 from Olden-

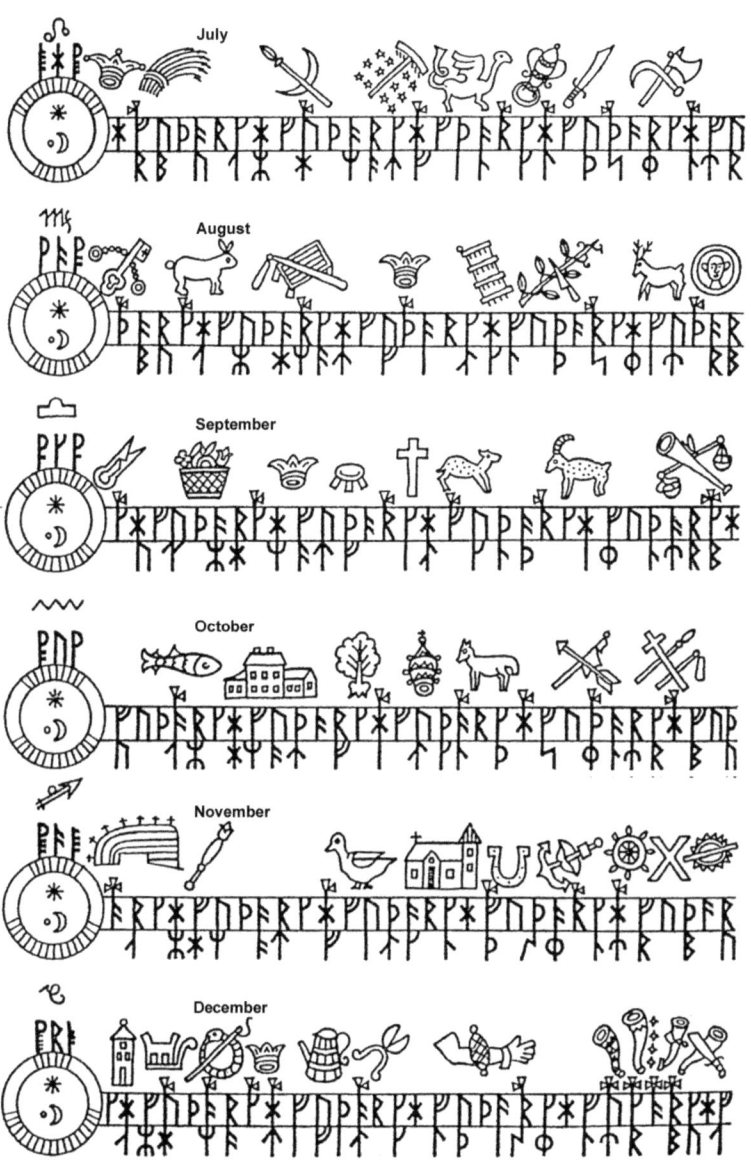

burg based on an original from 1743.

Fig. 33: Almanac.

In the Almanacs find three rows of symbols; at the top there are pictures that indicate the work of farmers during the year or characterize the festivals of the year, holy days, etc. In the middle row we only find the first seven runes of the younger runic alphabet, one after the other. These represent the days of the week. In the bottom row of each month there are runes too, apparently randomly distributed. These are the 16 runes of the younger runic alphabet, but extended by three runes; 19 runes were needed for the "Golden Number" to determine the phases of the moon. These additional three runes are actually bind runes, namely "arlaug", a combination of the Ár rune with the Lǫgr rune, then "tvimaðr" which means "two Maðr runes", lastly "bælgþorn" which means "double Thorn rune".

To determine the days of the week we only have to know which day of the week is the 1st January of the year. We can see the Fé rune in the middle row of the 1st January. Is it, for instance, a Thursday, then all Fé runes of the middle rows of the entire calendar are Thursdays, all Úr runes are Fridays etc.

To find out on which date a black moon or a full moon falls, we just have to divide the year of the respective year by 19, because after 19 years the full moon falls on the same day of the week. The remainder of this division indicates the numerical value of that rune in the bottom row on whose assigned weekday of the middle row a black moon is. If you add two weeks (14 days), you come to the rune in the middle row, where the full moon is.

Let's take 2021 as an example. January 1 of 2021 is a Friday; so all Fé runes in the middle row of the calendar are Fridays. To determine the moon we divide the year: 2021: 19 = 106, remainder 7. The seventh rune in the younger runic alphabet is the Hagall rune. Wherever is a Hagall rune in the bottom row, there is black moon (when the moon is invisible, before the new moon appears). For example, in January this rune appears below a Kaun rune. The Kaun rune is wednesday in 2021; it is the 13th rune in the middle row. That means, on Wednesday, January 13th, 2021 there will be a black moon. 14 days later, on Wednesday, January 27, 2021, there will be a full moon. However, the calendar is designed for Scandinavia and the information is not as accurate as we are used to today. Since the full moon changes every 29.5 days, it not always falls on a date exactly, but sometimes between two days. So there is an inaccuracy of ½ to 1 day. The full moon will appear on January 28th, as we know.

The rings at the beginning of each month show symbols on the inside, for day and night, sun and moon. The notches in the rings above the sun symbol indicate the number of the hours of the day; the notches below the moon symbol indicate the hours of the night. Above the rings there is a rune for calculating the day of the week, in front of and behind are stave numbers; these are runic numbers. Round arcs on such a number represent the "5", the single short lines each represent a "1". In January, the number "9" appears first on the left and the number "4" on the right. These numbers indicate the time of sunrise and sunset, above you can see the zodiac symbol. Everything is calculated for Scandinavian conditions. At the end of the Almanac the whole runic alphabet and the stave numbers for the annual calculation follow (not included in my illustration).

In the small pictures above the row of weekday runes we find small crosses or half-crosses that mark certain saints' days. We often see drinking horns because there was a lot of drinking at the festivals. The symbols themselves are self-explanatory, for example the fool's cap on February 2nd for the candlelight and carnival parades, the key at the end of February is a Peter's festival. The ship symbol at the beginning of April is the beginning of the shipping in spring, the harrow behind it shows the harrowing of the fields. At the end of the month there is the Easter lamb. In May we find the washtub for the May bath, a symbol for the May Queen, and the bishop's hat for Pentecost. On June 21 we recognize the midsummer tree, the beginning of the hay mowing at the beginning of July, the key with the chain for Lammas (Petri chain celebration) at the beginning of August, the flail, the pruning by the vintners and a deer as a sign of the beginning of the hunt. The cross in September represents parish fairs; the scales at the end of September indicate the autumn equinox, the Michaelmas, and the conclusion of old transactions. The cemetery at the beginning of November represents All Saints' Day, All Souls' Day (Halloween), the goose on November 11th is St. Martin's goose, the X at the end is the St. Andrew's Cross for St. Andrew's Night. In December we see an arm with a spindle, as now the time begins when it is no longer allowed to spin. The four large drinking horns represent Christmas.

In the meantime there are further insights. Since 1983 it is known that the 13 Heavenly Castles of the gods (in the 12 Eddaverses Grímnismál 4-8 and 11-17) are related to the signs of the zodiac and astrological houses. The museum in Reykjavík (Iceland) also shows a corresponding model of the cosmic worldview of the Vikings. The stanzas are neither rearranged nor the order of the constellations of the zodiac changed. Each Grímnismál stanza is assigned to a constellation of the zodiac, but in today's counting of the year with only 12 months, the 13th Heavenly Castle must be disregarded. Our ancestors counted the months from full moon to full moon and therefore they had to add an additional 13th month every 2-3 years. This additional month was connected to 13th Heavenly Castle of the god Ullr.

In addition to these one millennium old traditions of the zodiac or the circle of gods, the two millenium old runic alphabet perfectly fits to the 12 constellations of the zodiac and 12 months if you place the runes backwards in the year circle, with two runes per zodiac sign. The runes refer to the gods of the zodiac, or to the planetary rulers of the constellations, or to the seasonal festivals. May be this can help us to find out the oldest rune meanings, too.

Now one can ask: For what you need something like that? Well, we can find the deities who are important for us by looking at our ascendant and our sun sign and see which deities are there. Important planets in your own natal chart can also be significant. In each sign there is a god and a goddess, so that there are deities for men and women they can identify with. There are two runes for each constellation so that the position of our ascendant and our sun determines two runes that we can consider as runes that are relevant to us. We can also practice a Germanic astrology, because every planet has its rune, too:

Mercury	= ᚠ Fehu;	Saturn	= ᚦ Thorn;
Venus	= ᛒ Berkanan;	Sun	= ᛋ Sowelo;
Mars	= ᛏ Tiwaz;	Moon	= ᛗ Mannaz.
Jupiter	= ᚨ Ansuz;		

The classifications of Mars, Jupiter and Saturn are given by the Icelandic rune poem. The sun and moon are of course determined by the corresponding runes. I assign Venus, in due to the tradition of Freyja, to the birch rune, and Mercury to Fehu according to my interpretation. So you can add the runes of the planets of your own natal chart to a horoscope formular (Fig. 34) and set them in relation to the runes of the annual cycle and to the deities of the respective sign.

Placing an old system of cultic symbols in the cycle of the year must inevitably generate contradictions. For example, we don't find the rune of Venus (Berkanan) in a Venus constellation (that would be Taurus and Libra).

But now we come to the castles of the gods, the runes and constellations of the zodiac. I start with Fig. 34 on the left, in the middle.

Trudheim – Aries, Thor and Sif, runes Tiwaz and Berkanan. Aries starts at the equinox, the time when our ancestors celebrated Easter. This festival focuses on Ostara (an epithet of the goddess Freyja), Thor and Tyr. Berkanan is Ostara's (Freyja's) rune, and Tiwaz is the rune of the god Tyr. Easter was associated with a Thing (governing assembly), and since ancient times the god Tyr-Mars has also been the god of Things. On this Thing the young warriors were taken into the warrior clans and consecrated with birch branches (Berkanan). Also at Easter the girls were beaten lightly by the boys with birch rods, which was called "Oster-Stiepen" in Germany. Aries is a constellation of Mars, which corresponds to the rune of Tyr (= Mars). The month of March is named after Mars.

Alfheim – Taurus, Freyr and Gerdr, runes Algiz and Sowelo. These runes are both related to the sun, fitting the old German month

124

Fig. 34: The annual circle of zodiac, gods and runes with the annual festivals.

name "Sonnmond" (= Sun-moon) or Nordic "Sól" and the god Freyr who is a god of sun fire. Algiz represents the deer of the sun. We find the reference to Freyr in the myth that Freyr killed the winter giant Beli with a deer antler. In Celtic myths the god himself is the bearer of deer antlers (Cernunnos). Gerdr, on the other hand, represents the earth which is the element of Taurus, an earth sign. But the bull also represents fertility in a special way and therefore it is suitable for the fertility god Freyr. And the deer can also be a horned hind, which represents the earth in the myth: Sigrdrifa (the earth in spring) sleeps on "Hindarfjall" (hind mountain). The ruler of Taurus is Venus, i.e. Freyja. In fact, many love customs are passed down in the May Festival, such as the "Mailehen" (the auctioning off young women at a May festival), which fit the goddess of love and her brother Freyr. And Freyr is god of wealth, matching the second astrological house which gives information about property.

We have to neglect the Heavenly Castle of the god Ullr, Ydalir, as it was only needed for the 13th lunar month.

Valascialf – Twins, Vali and Sol, runes Eiwaz and Pertho. Vali is one of the two divine brothers, Vidar and Vali, who are mentioned in ancient mythology as the twins Castor and Pollux, matching the constellation of the twins. Since the divine brothers court the sun (according to Indian and Baltic myths), the goddess of the sun is suitable here. And both brothers represent the return of the gods after the great end of the world (ragnarök, doomsday), which is related to the Pertho rune. It also means "children" and both brothers are children of the gods and are depicted as young boys. Therefore the third astrological house also provides information about siblings and relatives. Their father Odin is represented here in the planetary ruler of Mercury; his heavenly throne, Hlidskialf, is located in this Heavenly Castle, the highest point of the sun in summer. The Eiwaz rune just after the summer solstice refers to the hidden attack on the god Balder who was shot by the mistletoe at midsummer. In the north the rune is also called "Stuppmadr" (fallen man) ⋏, and both runes have something to do with death and rebirth, which fits the name of the Heavenly Castle, Valascialf, provided that the connection with Val = death, Valhall = realm of the dead is recognized here.

Söcqvabecq – Cancer, Odin and Saga, runes Isaz and Jeran. Even the symbol of the Cancer in classical astrology with the two crabs ♋ reminds of the Jeran rune with its two halves ◊. It shows the divided year, and we now are exactly at the point of the summer solstice. Until today in this festival the divided annual cycle is represented as a midsummer tree (see Fig. 32, p. 118 below). Two deities are named here, Odin and his daughter Saga, who represent the intimate family life about which the 4th astrological house provides information. In the midsummer tradition, springs and fountains are also decorated, matching the name of the sky castle, which means "Sink-stream" and matching the goddess Saga or Laga, who also has something to do with water-sources. The Isaz rune doesn't seem to be a good fit, but it is also described as a "river bark" and bridge over a water, fitting the name Söcqvabecq. Ice is also frozen water, which symbolizes the element of cancer.

Gladsheim – Leo, Bragi and Idunn, Runes Hagla and Naudiz. In the Edda Bragi and Idunn are not mentioned to live in this castle, but we know from the poems (Eireksmál, Hákonarmál) that Bragi greets the deceased in Valhalla. During this time the old festival of the linen harvest was celebrated, which is also called "Hagelfest" (= hail festival) in German customs, matching the Hagla rune, to protect the harvest from hailstorms. The lighted fires there are the need-fires (Nydfyr), matching the Naudiz rune, which perhaps also means the beginning of the hay mowing. The Hagla rune in the Edda rune song also represents protection from fire, and also for Valhalla as a protected place. The ruler of the sign Leo is the sun, embodied in the god Odin, who undoubtedly also includes solar aspects. His eye is a symbol for the sun.

Thrymheim – Virgo, Loki and Skadi, Runes Gebo and Wunjo. The 6th astrological house provides information on diseases; the name of the giant-descended goddess Skadi means "damage, harm", fitting the Nordic month of August, "Skurdar", which refers to the grain harvest. The ruler of the Virgin, Mercury, is expressed by the myth that Skadi had a connection with Odin, as well as by the Wunjo rune, which implies Odin as a wish-fulfiller. It is height of the summer when the grain is harvested, which in the myth is represented by Loki cutting off the hair of the goddess Sif. If the Wunjo rune represents an ear of wheat, then it is very suitable here, while the Gebo rune is also a symbol for a festival of sacrifice, because the autumn festival is celebrated at the end of the constellation of the Virgin. The Celts call this rune the "Cross of Lugh", and the name Lugh is etymologically related to Loki, although Lugh is considered a main god of the Celts, different from Loki.

Breidablic – Libra, Baldr and Nanna, runes Raido and Kenaz. It is the time from the equinox of autumn when the light god Baldr sinks into the underworld, followed by his wife Nanna, because now the nights are longer than the days, the dark predominates and the light is located in the underworld (it will return six months later). The symbol of the scales also refers to the autumn equinox itself, where day and night are of equal length, i. e. "balanced". And it is said that Baldr's judgment cannot stand because his judgments are so balanced. The way of Baldr and Nanna into the underworld is represented by the Raido rune, the Kenaz rune means the karma of sinking and later return of the gods. But this rune is also a rune of the Kienfackel (pine wood torch), because from the autumn equinox people had to light a light in the houses because it gets dark earlier. This rune, interpreted in the sense of "ashes", can also be related to the burial of Baldr and Nannas (cremation). The seventh astrological house is traditionally called "the setting" and refers to husbands (Nanna, Baldr's wife) and enemies (Hödr, Baldr's enemy). The ruler of the sign is the planet Venus, here probably represented by Nanna, because Nanna is a goddess of dawn and evening red like Inanna of the the Sumerians, therefore she voluntarily follows the god of light and day, Baldr, like the evening follows the fading day.

Himinbiorg – Scorpio, Heimdall and Var, runes Thorn and Ansuz. Thorn is the death thorn of winter, the time at which the giants let the earth fall asleep. The image of the scorpion is a reminder of it, because this animal has the poisonous sting, analogous to the death thorn of the rune. During the time of the Scorpio the old festival of the dead and the beginning of winter are also celebrated, which is the Christians call All Saints' Day (all hallows even, Halloween). The saints in Christianity represent the same as the gods and spirits (the Aesir) do in paganism. And here we can actually find the rune Ansuz, the rune of the Aesir and the god Odin. Perhaps this rune here also represents the planetary ruler Mars, because in old sources Odin is sometimes compared with Mars because he also directs the battles. Heimdall is the guardian of the heavenly bridge to the gods, actually guardian at the entrance to the realm of the dead, who lets the souls (Ansuz) pass or rejects them. The eighth astrological house is called "the upper gate" because it is the gate at the entrance to the kingdom of gods. The sky bridge is also identified with the Milky Way, which is also called "Iringsweg" (Rigs Way,

Heimdalls Way) and which cuts the zodiac at that place where the constellations of Scorpio and Sagittarius are. That is why the eighth astrological house is the house of death, which also provides information about legacies.

Folcvang – Sagittarius, Odr and Freyja, runes Fehu and Uruz. In the Edda the Uruz rune is also called the "entrance door", which can then refer to the entrance to the kingdom of gods at the end of the sky bridge, because the Milky Way partly goes through Sagittarius. But Uruz is also a rune of the earth goddess and may represent Freyja, too. In this case Fehu would be the rune of Odr, Freyja's husband. Some people see Odr as just an incarnation of the god Odin, which would suit the Fehu rune and the ruler of the constellation, Jupiter. Other people see Odr as Hodr, the god who shoots Baldr with the mistletoe, which fits the Sagittarius. We can also imagine Freyja with the bow as the leader of the Valkyries; she is shown with an arch on the bracteate of Eschwege-Niederrhone (7th century). The Swedish rune researcher Johannes Bureus (early 17th century) even wanted to consider the rune Fehu as Freyja's rune. In any case, Freyja receives half of the dead and therefore she is also a goddess of the dead, suitable for the Uruz rune as the entrance to the afterlife and suitable for winter. The Fehu rune as Odin's rune fits the "wild hunt" of this time of year and the customs on St. Nicholas Day, when Rupprecht (= Odin) roams. But the rune was also related to the god Freyr, who – like Odin – was and is worshiped in the beginning of Yule (Christmas, the winter solstice). Incidentally, the Sagittarius (i.e. the group of stars that creates the arrow of Sagittarius) aims precisely at the center of our galaxy, just as the Scorpio's stinger does.

Glitnir – Capricorn, Forseti and Syn, runes Dagaz and Othala. The rune Othala as a rune of our own yard and home still relates to

Christmas, which lasted 12 days and therefore extends into this constellation. The main parts of the festival were celebrated in the house; the people cultivated peace and comfort in their own home. Perhaps this is also a reference to loneliness and isolation that the planetary ruler Saturn causes here. The goddess Syn protects the house and its inhabitants and is also a goddess who protects the defendants, like the god of law Forseti. Syn, as the sister of the sun, also has references to the sun and the fire of the hearth. Forseti fits this time because it is the time period after the winter solstice which was the time period after the battle of the gods against the giants. Now the dispute is decided and therefore the god of law fits here. He is also the son of Baldr and so he is the god of light and day. Another name for Baldr is Dagr, old english Bael-daeg (day), and the Dagaz rune is found in this constellation. The Dagaz rune emerged from the wheel cross ⊗ (⊗ changed to ⊠ and then to ⋈), a symbol of the sun and the day; the days are getting longer again now.

Noatun – Aquarius, Njordr and Njorunn, runes Laguz and Ingwaz. The laguz rune, the rune of water in every form, stands for the god of the sea Njordr and his wife Njorunn. The other rune is the Ingwaz rune. Ing (Freyr) is the son of Njord and therefore he fits here, especially since the carnival festival is celebrated at this time, which was once especially for the god Ing (Frøblót). The procession of the goddess Njorunn (Nerthus), which the Roman Tacitus described, also took place in spring, i.e. at this time. The laguz rune also represents the meltwater of the snow.

Landvidi – Pisces, Vidar and Snotra, runes Ehwaz and Mannaz. According to the myth the god Vidar sits alone on the back of the horse to wait for the time when he has to avenge his father. The horse is represented by the Ehwaz rune. The god kills the fenris wolf, that's vengeance. This wolf represents the winter darkness, and after the constellation of the Pisces the spring equinox follows, from where the days become longer than the nights and the light triumphs over the dark. The Mannaz rune seems to be less suitable here, may be it represents the creation of humans in the beginning of the year or the goddess Freyja as the moon goddess who was worshiped both, at Carnival and at Easter.

Even in classical astrology, 5 of the 12 constellations are not animals at all, and all constellations represent deities. The term "zodiac" for the circle of gods is therefore inappropriate and slightly derogatory, which is why occultists used the term "Tyrkreis" (= Tyr circle) at the beginning of the last century. Because the god Tyr (Tius) stands in the center of the circle at the zenith, the circle rotating around him. The north star, which our ancestors associated with Tyr, has its place here today as two rune songs for the Tiwaz rune still explain. In the center below is the earth, Fria (Frigg), in her realm Fensalir. However, Fria is not only the earth goddess, but also the sky goddess, and the lower dome of the sky is assigned to her.

By the way, our ancestors also knew the two lunar nodes, i.e. the intersections of the lunar orbit with the ecliptic. The ascending lunar knot or dragon's head represents the zeitgeist, similar to the Capricorn according to Agrippa. The descending lunar knot or dragon's tail works against the zeitgeist, similar to the Scorpion according to Agrippa. The Indians call the first one Rahu, the other one Ketu and interpret both negatively. The name Ketu, however, is etymologically related to the name Hati (we also find the K to H change in the Hagla rune). In Germanic mythology, there are two wolves, Skoll and Hati, who chase the sun and moon and symbolize the two lunar nodes. That two wolves chases the stars and that one of them bears the name of an Indo-European lunar knot, are proof that Germanic people knew and practiced astrology, and the Germanic interpretation corresponds to the Indian one, because both wolves are rather evil in myth. The book Picatrix (around 1055 C.E.) explains the two lunar nodes as follows:

"And know that the nature of the head [ascending lunar knot, Skoll] is multiplication: if it is in conjunction with the happy planets, then it increases their happiness-bringing power; but if it is in conjunction with the unlucky planets, then it increases their unhappy power. The tail [descending lunar knot, Hati], on the other hand, is of a diminishing nature: if it is in conjunction with the planets of happiness, then it diminishes their auspicious power; if it is in conjunction with the unlucky planets, it diminishes their unhappy power."

Another proof is the naming of the weekday names. The Germanic people are said to have taken over the days of the week from the Romans and replaced the names of the Roman deities with Germanic ones. This happened before the 4th century. It is noticeable that they did not find a Germanic deity for Saturn. The Roman mythological Saturn was worshiped as the god of wealth, agriculture, abundance and the Golden Age. So it would have been appropriate to replace him with the god Ing (Yngvi-Freyr), the god of fertility and wealth, but that did not happen. Why not? Because they also knew the astrological Saturn, which means the great misfortune as well as rigidity, old age, cold and death. That would not have been suitable for the young and life-affirming god Ing. The Germanic people wanted to keep the astrological meanings and not just replace names.

Chapter 13

Runic inscriptions

Here at the end of this book I want to show some runic inscriptions of our ancestors. When transferring runic inscriptions, the runes are transferred with their phonetic values for easier readability (see table Fig. 3, p. 15).

The rune stone from Rö, Bohuslän, Sweden, early 5th century, has the longest runic inscription from the Iron Age. The 2 meters (6.5 feet) high stone is now located in the Stockholm Museum; there is now a copy at its discovery place on the farm. This inscription can be found on four parallel lines on the stone:

ek hrazaz satido [s]tain	„I, Hrar, set the stone
swabaharjaz anai ....r	Swabahari the ...
s.irawidaz	with wide wounds
staina warijaz fahido	Stonewarrior colored".

The inscription with 68 runes, some of them are not legible (indicated here with dots, the S rune has been added because it was very likely to be here), is unclear. Is "Swabahari" ("the Suebi High") the deceased who died of his wounds? "Hrar" ("stirrer") is the stone setter; but is "Stainawari" a proper name of the rune master or does it just mean "guardian stone", a protective stone against grave destroyers?

In 1880 and 1883, two rune stones, the stones Tørvika A and B, were found in the relics of a long looted large stone grave in Tørvika, Hordaland, Norway. Stone A has the inscription:

(e)k la(n)da warijaz   „I, the country guardian".

To get the magical number of 12 runes, the rune carver omitted the rune sounds in brackets. The inscription was supposed to protect the grave against harm, which hadn't worked. Or it refers to a eminent dead person, but the inscription on the second stone indicates the first possibility, because it says:

heþro dwen...g k   „Get out of here, G K"

In the inscription there is the Th rune, transferred with the symbol þ. Three runes are illegible. The text is probably directed against a grave robber who, with the help of the term runes Gebo and Kenaz ("gift of illness"), should be cursed by these runes to fall ill.

On the stone from Möjbro (Møjebro), Uppland, Sweden, 5th century (Fig. 35) there is the inscription in three lines, starting right-to-left and from the bottom:

frawaradaz ana hahai slagina z

"Frawarad slain on the Runner" (reading by Prof. Dr. Wolfgang Krause).
"Frawarad Ane the one-eyed slain" (reading by Otto von Friesen).

The proper name Frawarad means "who gives quick advice". Is that the dead man or is that Ane?

A horseman with a shield and sword can be seen on the stone; Below we can see the relicts of two animals, probably dogs. The interpretation of the inscription is unclear, as two names are mentioned and probably only one of them was buried here.

Abb. 35: Stone from Möjebro or Hagby, Uppland, Sweeden.

If Frawarad is the dead man who was slain on the "Renner" (= Runner, a horse), why is he shown riding? Would we today depict someone sitting in a car who died in a car accident? And if the other interpretation is correct that a certain one-eyed Ane is the deceased, who is Frawarad then? The rider with the two dogs could also be the god Woden, because the dogs could be Woden's wolves Geri and Freki, and the horse is also an attribute of Woden. But then the spear, which is one of Woden's oldest attributes, would be missing. After all, it is interesting that the condition of monocular vision is mentioned, because Woden is also one-eyed. So it is possible that "Frawarad" or "Ane" is an unknown nickname for Woden who is said to accompany the slain dead here.

The arrangement of the rune lines is strange on the 2.45 meters high stone. While the name is placed well in the middle in the lower row, the second part of text is above it, and there was not enough space for the last rune, so it was placed on top of it separate. This last rune is the Algiz rune, and this is a good protective rune. So maybe it is no coincidence that that rune has a prominent place there. I calculated the key rune of the whole inscription (see Chapter 10) and came up with 8, remainder 24, i.e. the Othala rune and perhaps the Wunjo rune. So the dead should enjoy delights in the new home.

Stone from Vetteland, Rogaland, Norway, around 400. Two fragments of this presumed tombstone have been found; a third one is missing, so that the inscription is incomplete:

...flagdafakinaz ist   „threatened by fiends
...magoz minas staina   my son's Stone
...daz faihido   (name)...daz painted".

138

Stone from Reistad, Agder, Norway, around 500:

iuþingaz ek wakraz unnam wraita
„Juthing. I, Wakr, did the writing".

"Juthing" can be the name of the deceased; it is less likely that a particular Thing place or tribe was referred to. "Wakr" means "the waking", and since "Vakr" is also a name of Woden, it probably indicates an initiation in which the initiate consecrated himself to Woden and had to stay awake for a certain time period (three days) to bring about visions. This rune master has obviously done that and was therefore entitled to use the name "Wakr". The Ehwaz rune can only be seen as a vertical line, i.e. half; and it is noticeable that the Ingwaz rune was not used, but the Naudiz and Gebo runes instead. In the word "unnam" there are also two identical runes standing next to each other, which is rare.

Stone from Saude, Telemarken, Norway, around 500:

wadaradas   „of the Wandarad".

The stone is lost and nothing is known about the exact circumstances of the find, which is why its date is uncertain. The name "Wandarad" means "who takes on what causes difficulties". The end of the name shows the Sowelo rune instead of the Algiz rune; the last S / Z sound had not become an R at that time.

Belland Stone, Vest-Agder, Southern Norway, around 500:

keþan   „of the Ketha" (name)

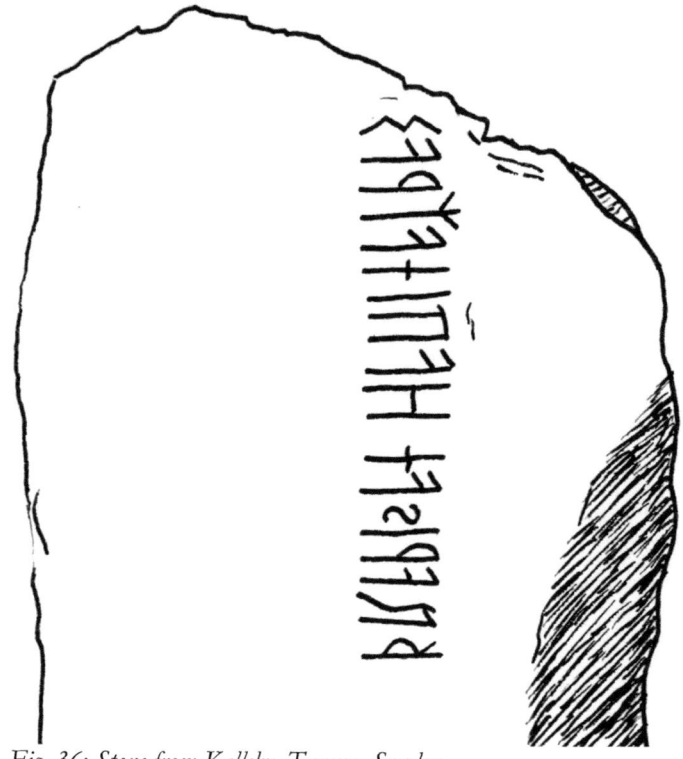

Fig. 36: Stone from Kalleby, Tanum, Sweden.

Stone from Kalleby, Tanum, Bohuslän, Sweden, around 400 (Fig. 36):

þrawijan haitinazwas   „Promised to the Thrawinge".

The name Thrawinge means "to yearn" and it is said to be a divine name of the god Ing-Fro (Yngvi-Freyr), so that a worshiper with the inscription determined the flat stone slab as the sacrificial altar of the god Ing. The 3 meters high stone is located outdoors, but its original location is no longer known.

Stone from Stenstad, Telemark, Norway, between 410-440:

igijon h̲alaz   „To the Igijo Hall ".

The runes H and A are a bind rune. The stone stood on a large burial mound of a woman's grave, so that the inscription will refer to the woman buried. The 63 cms high, round stone was given away to Denmark, where it still stands today at the Jægerspris hunting lodge on Zealand.

Stone from Skärkind, Östergötland, Sweden, around 450:

ski(n)þa leubaz   „Fur-Leubar".

Instead of "fur" we can also translate "skin", and "Leubar" seems to be a proper name here, which means "lover". You can also recognize this name on the stone from Järsberg, Värmland, Sweden:

[?]ubaz h[a]ite: h̲arabanaz   „? was my name, Raven
h̲ait[eka] ek e̲rilaz runoz waritu   is my name, I, the Eruler
                                     carved the runes".

Because runes were missing at the beginning, the runes "ubaz" were added to "leubaz", while others were added to "eagle owl" or "hooded bird" ("hubaz"). H-A and E-R are bind runes; the Erilaz is the rune master. With "eagle owl" the text makes more sense (reference to an initiation) than if we start from the name Leubar.

Stone of Barmen, Vestland, Norway, 400-450:

ek þirbijaz ru   „I, spoil ru(nes)"
Add something like: "I, the Corrupter, painted the runes". But the

name can also simply be a proper name "Terbes son"; and whether the last runes "ru" may be added to the word "runes" is questionable. The key rune is the 15th Algiz rune, the protective rune.

Opedal stone, Hardanger, Norway, first half of the 5th century:

birgŋgu b<u>uuruu</u> swestar minu mez wage
„Rescue site. Home in peace, sister, my dear, go away ".

The symbol "ŋ" represents the Ingwaz rune. This inscription seems to be directed against the deceased sister as a revenant. Revenants are deads who return to the living and bring calamity.

Stone from Einang, Valdres, Norway, 2nd half of the 4th century:

(ek go)daga(s)tiz runo faihido   „(I, Go)dguest painted runes".

The bracketed letters are additions from the interpreters. The rune carver could also have had a different name.

Stone from Vånga, Västergötland, Sweden, early 6th century:

haukoþuR   „The hawk-Odur".

The hawk (old north. haukr) is one of the sacred birds of the god Woden, perhaps also of the god Odur. It is related to the name of the god Odur (Odr), the consort of the goddess Freyja, the flat stone (as an altar?) may have been dedicated to.

Stone from Myklebostad, Romsdal, Norway, 2nd half of the 6th century:

asugasdiR [hl]aiwa aih iþroti litil(o) orumalaib[aR]

„Aesirguest burial mound. Worm-life has little skill".

„Aesirguest" could be a name, or it indicates that the dead will be a guest of the Aesir (gods). "Worm life" could be the rune carver then.

Stone from Krogsta, Uppland, Sweden, early 6th century. (Fig 37):

mwsëeij
s1/1ainaz

The inscription is unclear and partly illogical. On the stone side we can certainly read "stai-nar" (stone), but the Tiwaz rune is encoded as a hook rune: One hook stands for the group, another one for the rune in the group, i.e. group 1, rune 1 = Tiwaz (the three rune groups are counted backwards, so the 1st group begins with Tiwaz). But what kind of name is hid-den behind the inscription on

Fig. 37: Stone from Krogsta.

the front of the stone? Why is there the Eiwaz rune ("ë") with the sound "ei" and then the runes separately again? Or is this Eiwaz rune just a 1/1 hook rune for Tiwaz: "mwsteij"? The figure is sup-posed to discourage grave robbers.

Whetstone from Strøm, Norway around 600:

wate h̲ali hino hor̲na̲
ha̲ ha̲ skaþi ha̲þu ligi

"Water this stone, horn!
Sickle, harm! Beheaded lie down".

The whetstone (grindstone) was carried in a horn filled with water.
He is supposed to damage (grind) the sickle so that the mowing
lies. The word "skathi" (= harm) is also the name of the goddess
Skadi. The first line (maybe also the second) is an old work song.

Stone from Haverslund, Øster Løgum, Denmark, around 900 (Fig.
38). In younger runes it only says (read from bottom to top):

hairulfR
„Army wulf".

It is an epithet of Woden and an old name, already found on a helmet B from Negau (5th century BC): "to the god Hariguest" (=
guest in the army). Prince Friedrich-Karl of Prussia had the stone
brought to Berlin on the 1864 campaign and placed it in front of
the Dreilinden hunting lodge. Today it is back in Denmark.

Stone from Tune, Norway, around 400 AD (Fig. 39, p. 146):

[me]z woduride staina	„For me, Woduri the Stone
þrijoz dohtriz d̲alidun	three daughters prepare
arbij asijostez arbijano	the inheritance next the Aesir
ek wiwaz after woduri	I, Wiwaz after Woduri
de wita̲da̲ h̲alaiban worahto	worked, my employer".

The name of the deceased is "Woduri", that means "Ragerider", which is also a Wodens cult name. Woduri may have been a Wodens priest. Wiwaz ("the consecrated") was his successor, who was probably initiated by Woduri in a fasting ritual. This is what the term "employer" indicates, because we know from the rune song of the Edda (Háv. 139) a similar formulation at Woden's own initiation. The three daughters could be three daughters of Woduri, but it could also be a mythological reference to the three women of fate, the Norns.

Vehlingen Cup, Rees District, Lower Rhine, before the 1st century:

tiiiu   „Tius" (Deity).

This runic inscription used to be regarded as the oldest runic inscription, today the scientists only wants to recognize "pre-runic conceptual symbols" in it and it does not rank among the runes, despite the complete equality of the symbols with the runes.

Brooch (clasp) from Meldorf, around 50 AD:

hiwi   „for Hiwi" (womanname).

It is considered the oldest runic inscription by researchers today.

Spear shaft from Kragehuler Moor, Funen, Denmark, 350-550:

ek erilaz asugisalas mu ha haite ga ga ga ginunga helija haga-la wiju bi g(aiza)

145

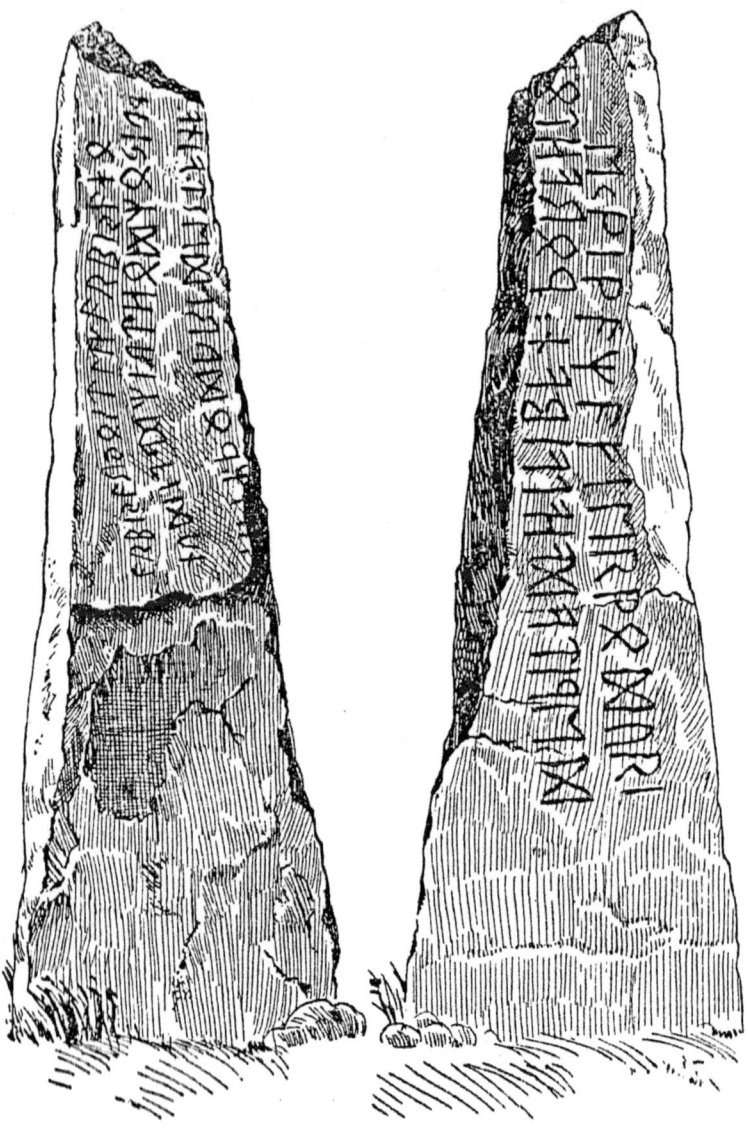

Fig. 39: The runestone from Tune.

"I, the Eruler (rune master) of the Aesir descendant, am called Muha, Gebo-Ansuz, Gebo-Ansuz, Gebo-Ansuz. I consecrate holy hail on the spear".

The inscription is interpreted very differently, the runes Gebo-Ansuz are also interpreted as abbreviations for "gibu auja" (give luck), they are bind runes. The spear is supposed to destroy the enemy with hail.

Spearhead from Kovel, Volhynia, 3rd century:

tilarids   „Target rider".

To this spear was given a name, and "Targetrider" also contains the name of the Raido rune that Woden uses in the Edda to inhibit an arrow. The inscription is right-to-left, and there are also magical symbols on the spearhead.

Spearhead from Dahmsdorf (Müncheberg), Brandenburg, 3rd century:

ranja   „Against runner".

This inscription is also right-to-left, and there are further magical symbols on the tip. The name is probably identical to the nickname Wodens, "Rani". So the warrior wanted to use Woden's power for his spear.

The right-to-left inscriptions should correspond to the direction of flight of the spears, but also be indefinable for strangers.

Bracteate (magic pendant) No. 22 from Vadstena and bracteate embossed with the same stamp from Motala, Östergötland, Sweden 1st half of the 6th century (Fig. 40):

luwatuwa : fuþarkgw : hnijëbzs : tbemlŋo[d]

Fig. 40: Bracteate from Vadstena.

On this bracteate we first find an uninterpreted magic word "Luwatuwa" and the entire runic alphabet. The division into groups (aettir) is already recognizable by colons. Instead of the P rune Pertho the rune carver used the B rune, which has a similar sound. The D-rune at the end should be covered according to the scientists. It was found that the rune number is exactly 366 (days of the leap year). Depicted is a god's head above a horned mount and a raptor.

Bracteate No. 25 from Tjurkö, Blekinge, Sweden, 5th to 6th century (Fig. 41):

wurte   runoz   an   walhakurne heldaz kunimu(n)diu
"Worked runes on foreign grain Helda to Kunimund".

Here, too, the picture shows a god's head above a horned mount and a bird. The bracteates were worn as magical protective pendants and often carry runes, e.g. the magic word "alu" (Ansuz, Laguz, Uruz).

Fig. 41: Bracteate from Tjurkö.

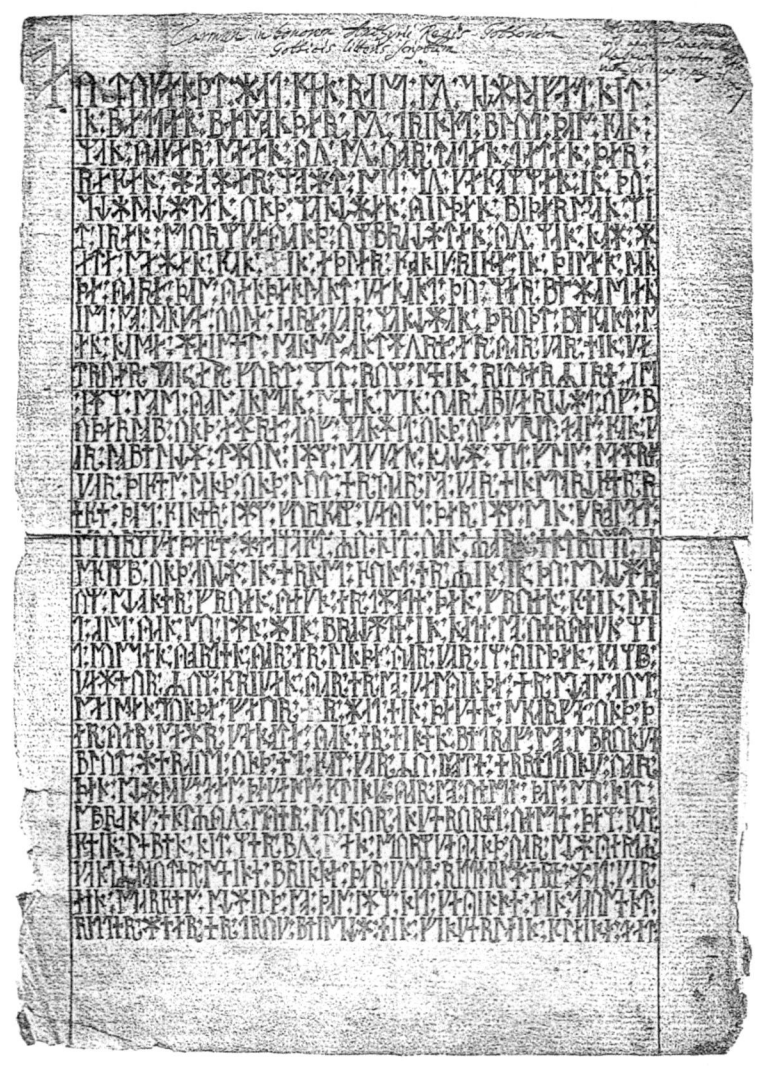

Fig. 42: The Doberan Anthyr song. A handwriting completely in runes.

In addition to the countless rune stones and rune inscriptions on objects, there are also some manuscripts completely in younger runes. The best known is the "Codex Runicus" (the law of Scania) from the end of the 13th century.

Fig. 42 shows one of them, sheet 1 of the Doberan Anthyr song. Heinrich Langermann, prince instructor at the Mecklenburg court (d. 1651) had a copy of a manuscript written "in Gothic script", "in a wondrous way found several years ago in the Closter Dobberan in the principality of Meklenburg, by several imperial soldiers in a walled up secret cupboard" , which "of Anthyri, the king of the Vends, who was the founder of the highly praiseworthy Hertzoge of Mekelenburg" the song of praise sent. In the meantime, however, this manuscript is considered a forgery of the 17th century.

Fig. 43 shows the so called "Isruna treatise" from the Codex Bruxellensis 9565-9566 from the 9th century. In the manuscript we find at first the Anglo-Saxon runes with names and sound values as well as the Anglo-Saxon additional runes. But then various rune codes (secret runes) are explained, and examples of the latin name Corvi ("raven") are given. The codes themselves are always the same, whereby a small rune denotes the group (the aett); after a point there are large runes to indicate the number of the rune in the aett. So the K rune is the 6th rune in the 1st group, and in the encryption with Isaz runes it looks like this: ı.ııııı. In this system, the groups are counted from the beginning, that means the runes from Fehu are the first group. The other encodings are the same; only in the case of the Lago runes the Laguz runes are used for encryption. At the Hahal runes there are conifer-like characters with side branches, on the left for the group and on the right for the rune.

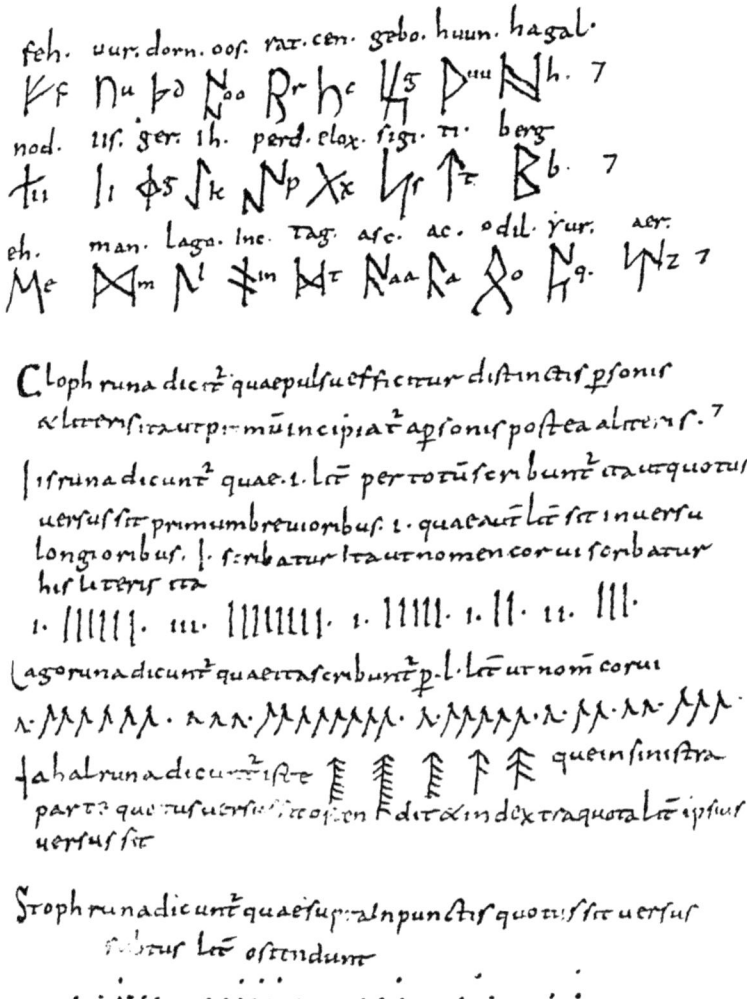

Fig. 43: Isruna treatise from the Codex Bruxellensis, 9th century.

The stophruna, i. e. point runes, explained below, are interesting. At the top there are one to three points for the group, at the bottom below we see the points for the run number in the group. Such a series of points, for example at the edge of a letter, is not recognizable as text for an ignorant person. So a secret can be passed on, provided the recipient knows the runes.

The clophruna, "knock runes", are even more ingenious. Here the group and the number in the group are conveyed by separate knockings (with a short interruption) or by knocking on different objects so that the knocking sounds different. These knocking runes are like Morse code; just easier to remember because they're more systematic. Such communications were used when cultic silence was ordered, e.g. later in the monasteries, but also in Paganism there were commands of silence; and even today young girls silently draw Easter water during the Easter Vigil. Prisoners in different cells could also communicate in this way without the guards noticing what the prisoners were communicating in this way.

Encodings continued by shifting runes. For example, somebody took always the following rune and encrypted it, but used was always the rune before it (or behind, depending on the system). In the example above, with the Isaz runes, the K rune would not be encrypted, but the Raido rune that is before the K rune in the row would be used. The first rune Fehu is called the 24th rune in this system, since there is no other rune before the first rune.

The encodings with group and rune number were also made with small images, for example faces with beards, whose left whiskers denote the group, the right whiskers denote the runes, or with vertically drawn fish or birds whose fins or wings denote the runes on the left and right.

152

Fig. 44: Runic ring from Körlin, Pomerania, Germany.

A good example of a magical rune ring can be found in the gold ring from Körlin, Kolberg district, Pomerania, Germany, 6th century (Fig. 44). In addition to the hammer sign of Thorr (swastika) for the consecration, the well-known word "alu" is written on another of the nine segments at the bottom in right-to-left reading direction. But above that we find a special sign, a rune composition. Above it is the Laguz rune, below the upside down Ansuz rune. But at the same time it is a secret rune. The hook at the top right describes the group, the two hooks at the bottom the rune in the group. Group 1, rune 2 is Uruz. So in this sign too we have Ansuz, Laguz and Uruz. The magical rune word ALU appears on inscriptions from the 3rd to the 8th century. The meaning is controversial; mostly the researchers interprets the word in the sense of "protection" (old english. ealgian), "amulet", "defense" (greek 'alké), "magic" (hittithic alwanzatar), or "to be beside oneself" (greek 'alyein).

At first glance, the interpretation as "beer" (old north. Ql) seems strange, because the old "alu" had to develop in the north to "olu" and could be shortened then to "ol" (Ql = beer). The explainer assume that a runic inscription was consecrated as an offering by pouring beer over it or that beer was sacrificed and drank for the success of the magic. In the Edda "Ølrúnar" are actually mentioned (Sigrdrifumál 7):

> *"You shall know Ølrúnar that the other's wife*
> *Doesn't betray you if you trust.*
> *Carv it on the horn and the back of the hand*
> *And draw Nauðr [n] on the nail."*

But whether these "beer runes" are really the former alu runes remains questionable.

We often find the word rearranged, e.g. as "lua" or shortened to "al". It has also been rearranged on the bracteate by Vadstena (p. 148) and expanded to include the Wunjo rune: "luwa ...".

The ancient Egyptians knew three related signs of salvation: Ankh (life), Udschat (salvation) and Senebu (health). Perhaps we have to interpret our "alu" in a similar way as a general salvation formula.

Photo credit

1: Wolfgang Krause, Was man in Runen ritzte, Halle 1935;
3, 5, 7, 12: Wikimedia Commons, Wikipedia;
4: Werner Brast (Hrsgb.), Mittelingsblatt für Vor- und Frühgeschichte, Berlin 1980;
6: Photo: Árpád v. Nahodyl Neményi;
8, 16: E. Doepler, W. Ranisch, Walhall – Die Götterwelt der Germanen, Berlin 1900;
9, 11, 28, 40: Helmut Arntz, Handbuch der Runenkunde, Halle 1944;
10, 13, 14, 15: Ludwig Gruber, Erschließung des Sinnzusammenhanges der Runenreihe auf Spuren einer urzeitlichen Glaubenswelt, Wien 1955;
17: Neuruppiner Bilderbogen von Oehmigke & Riemschneider, Reprint durch das Museum für Deutsche Volkskunde StMPK, Berlin o. J.;
19: Oskar Montelius, Kulturgeschichte Schwedens, Leipzig 1906;
22: Jon Arnason, Islenzkar Þióðsögur og Aevintyri, 1954;
26: UiO, Kulturhistorisk Museum, Oslo, Photo: Mårten Teigen;
29: A. v. Nahodyl Neményi, Liebesgöttin Freyja, Bad Belzig 2020;
25, 30, 34, 36, 37: Zeichnungen des Verfassers;
32: Karl Theodor Weigel, Runen und Sinnbilder, Berlin 1935;
33: Otto Sigfrid Reuter, Germanische Himmelskunde, München 1934;
35, 38, 39: Edmund Weber, Kleine Runenkunde, Berlin 1941;
41: F. Holthausen (Übers.), L. F. A. Wimmer, Die Runenschrift, Berlin 1887;
42: Abhandlungen der Kgl. Gesellschaft der Wissenschaften zu Göttingen, Bd. XL;
43: Otto Zeller, Der Ursprung der Buchstabenschrift und das Runenalphabet, Osnabrück 1977;
44: Rudolf John Gorsleben, Hoch-Zeit der Menschheit, Leipzig 1930.

Literature

Helmut Arntz, Handbuch der Runenkunde, Halle/Saale, 1935; 1944;
Sigurd Sierke, Kannten die vorchristl. Germanen Runenzauber? Königsberg 1939;
Konstantin Reichardt, Runenkunde, Jena 1936;
R. Derolez, Runica Menuscripta, Brugge 1954;
K. Düwel, Runenkunde, Sammlung Metzler, Stuttgart 1968;
Wolfgang Krause, Runen, Sammlung Göschen, Berlin 1970;
Edmund Weber, Kleine Ruinenkunde, Berlin 1941;
Ludwig Gruber, Erschließung des Sinnzusammenhanges der Runenreihe ...“ Wien 1955;
Géza von Neményi, Heilige Runen – Zauberzeichen dexs Nordens, Ullstein 2004.

Other books (in German)

Árpád v. Nahodyl Neményi, „Saemundar-Edda - Altnordisch", BoD 2019, 316 Seiten, ISBN 978-3-7494-4867-8, 16,80 €.

Árpád v. Nahodyl Neményi, „Die Jüngere Edda - Altnordisch und deutsch", BoD 2017, 188 Seiten, ISBN 978-3-7448-9974-1, 14,80 €.

Árpád v. Nahodyl Neményi, „Götterlieder der Edda - Altnordisch und deutsch", BoD 2017, 316 Seiten, ISBN 978-3-7448-1008-1, 16,80 €.

Árpád v. Nahodyl Neményi, „Heldenlieder der Edda - Altnordisch und deutsch", BoD 2017, 316 Seiten, ISBN 978-3-7528-5722-1, 16,80 €.

Géza v. Neményi, „Kommentar zu den Götterliedern der Edda – Teil 1, Die Odinslieder", Kersken-Canbaz-Verlag, Holdenstedt 2008, 250 Seiten, 20 teils farbige Abb., ISBN 978-3-89423-133-0, 29,80 €.

Géza v. Neményi, „Kommentar zu den Götterliedern der Edda – Teil 2, Die Thorslieder", Kersken-Canbaz-Verlag 2012, 151 Seiten, 26 teils farbige Abbildungen, ISBN 978-3-89423-133-0, 22,90 €.

Géza v. Neményi, „Kommentar zu den Götterliedern der Edda – Teil 3, Die Vanenlieder", Kersken-Canbaz-Verlag, Holdenstedt 2014, 221 Seiten, 11 Abbildungen, ISBN 978-3-89423-136-1, 27,80 €.

Árpád von Nahodyl Neményi, "Kommentar zur Jüngeren Edda", BoD 2016, ISBN 978-3-7431-8114-4, 19,80 €.

Árpád v. Nahodyl Neményi, „Der Ursprung biblischer Mythen – Die Enträtselung christlicher Glaubensvorstellungen", BoD 2015, 388 Seiten, 52 Abbildungen, ISBN 978-3-7347-7522-2, 16,80 €

Árpád v. Nahodyl Neményi, „Was unsere Märchen bedeuten – Deutung der bekanntesten Märchen aus der Sammlung der Gebrüder Grimm", BoD 2015, 470 Seiten, 96 Abbildungen, ISBN 978-3-7347-9796-5, 16,80 €

Árpád v. Nahodyl Neményi, „Goden – Die heidnischen Priester der Germanen", BoD 2016, 158 Seiten, 53 teils farbige Abbildungen, ISBN 978-3-7322-8352-1, 12,80 €.

Árpád v. Nahodyl Neményi, „Thors Hammer - Mythen, Überlieferungen, Erkenntnisse". BoD 2019. 124 Seiten, 37 teils farb. Abb., ISBN 978-3-7504-1389-4, 9,80 €.

We are looking for translators and publishers in UK and USA.
nahodyl@gmx.de